Become a Life Coach

Set Yourself Free to Build the Life and Business You've Always Wanted

*Mitch Matthews &
David Nadler*

Download the AudioBook and Action Guide Journal Free

Just to say thanks for downloading our book, we would like to give you the full audiobook and action guide journal 100% free!

visit http://trainingtobealifecoach.com/action

Become a Life Coach Contents

"Become A Life Coach: Setting You Free to Build the Life and Business You've Always Wanted"

Become A Life Coach: Setting You Free to Build the Life and Business You've Always Wanted

If you are reading this book, then you're interested in the concept of life coaching or business coaching. More importantly, you're intrigued by the idea of building a career out of helping people.

If you're like me… you want to have a positive impact on others. Heck, I bet it's more than that for you. I'm guessing you want to help dramatically change people's lives for the better!

You want to see people doing more of what they were put on the planet to do and less of the other stuff. I'm also guessing that the thought of making some money as you do this doesn't hurt either. It may not be your primary motivation… but, again, it's still important. And that's okay.

If this describes you… you are in the right spot.

This ebook was specifically designed to help YOU decide whether coaching is really right for you. So let's dive in!

Be ready…

We are going to ask some hard questions.

At the same time... you can rest easy because these are the very questions I wish someone had asked me before I got started as a coach.

If you're where I was when I first started investigating coaching in 2001, I was in a job that wasn't a great fit for me. I ended most days feeling like I was on the wrong track. Worse yet, I felt like I could see the track I was supposed to be on, but I just wasn't sure how to get there. And I'll be honest, I started to doubt whether I could or would ever be able to make the leap over to it.

Sound familiar?

If so... I bet you have some questions.

Are you looking at coaching as an opportunity to make more of an impact? Are you hoping that coaching could help you do something that will be more fulfilling and satisfying? Are you thinking that coaching might offer you more control over your life by providing some additional income in the short run or a more fulfilling and lucrative career in the long run?

Wherever you are currently... we love that you connected with us. You might be asking why? Well, we love to help people think through this decision. Again... You may still be asking... why?

First off, I need to confess that I have a somewhat "strange" personal goal. I want to help launch one million dreams in my lifetime. In order to see that happen, I want to create a movement of people who have powerful tools that will help others launch their dreams and do more of what they were put on the planet to do. As you can imagine, when I talk about my million dream goal and my idea for this movement, some people think that sounds a bit weird, but I'm guessing you don't.

Now, in full disclosure, I'll also admit that we offer The Coach Mindset™. It's an Elite Life Coach™ Training and Certification program™. In it, we teach people not only how to coach more effectively, but we also provide proven business strategies to help you launch your own coaching practice successfully. We've been wildly blessed to get to work with and help launch hundreds of coaches around the world. And honestly, we'd love for you to think about joining us. BUT… that's not what this book is about.

This book is about helping you decide whether becoming a life coach or a business coach is the right thing for you. We're not going to point you toward our program during this book. Nope.

Our goal is to help you think through the critical questions I wish someone had asked me as I was investigating the coaching industry. These are the questions I didn't know I needed to ask myself because they were in my blind spot. I didn't know what I didn't know. I started out blindly, and I wasted time and I wasted money.

I want to commend you for being more intentional than I was. By reading this book, you're going to save yourself time, effort, potential embarrassment and money!

I should warn you though. We've offered the core concepts that we cover in this book to thousands of people who have considered becoming a life coach as a hobby, a side job or a six-plus figure job. For some, the questions we asked made MANY decide that coaching wasn't for them. As they looked deep within themselves and when they got a real-world perspective on what it takes to be an effective coach, they decided it wasn't for them. They walked away.

Sometimes when people hear that, they ask me whether I consider that a failure. They hear about the thousands of people who decide NOT to become a coach after reading this and they wonder if I'm working against my "1 million dream" goal and my aspirations of launching a movement of people helping others. But I consider the fact that many have used the contents in the book to decide that coaching isn't for them as a complete success!

Why? That's easy.

Not everyone is supposed to become a coach. Everyone isn't a good fit for this type of work. If they're not supposed to be a coach, I want them to know right away so they don't waste time, effort or money. At the same time, if this is the perfect fit for someone, I want them to be able to move forward with bold and informed confidence and not waste time, effort or money as they do!

As I said, I want to see a movement of people who have powerful tools that will help others to do more of what they were put on the planet to do and less of what they weren't. Plus, if those people want to make coaching a revenue source, I want them to have the resources and strategies they need to set up a thriving and sustainable coaching practice.

Now I'll also offer one caveat. If these questions don't get you excited about coaching, you have your answer. Maybe coaching just isn't for you. I'll be the first one to admit that there are a lot of people who are interested in coaching, but they're just not cut out to become a life coach or a business coach. That's right! In fact, one of the primary reasons we wrote this book was to persuade people who wouldn't be a good fit for coaching to look elsewhere. As you can guess, not everyone is meant to be an Elite life coach. Since I've been training coaches for over a decade, I just don't want people to make an investment of time and money in becoming a coach, if it is eventually going to be a bad fit. If these questions don't click with you... no hard feelings. It just means that there is a very good chance that coaching isn't right for you. So... if that's the case, consider yourself set free to explore other things.

So that's it. Whether you choose to train with us or not... I'd love to help you in this process. Because I believe in you, and because I believe that if these questions confirm that coaching is right for you, you'll be able to become the coach you've always wanted to be!

Being Intentional...

Now, one of the things that you'll come to know about us is that we are intentional. I bet you are, too.

As a result... I have a suggestion for you on how to proceed with this ebook. My suggestion is to set some time aside to experience this. That's right. I said, "experience this." What do I mean? In our fast-paced world, we develop ways to take in information quickly. It's a defense mechanism that we've all developed over time due to the barrage of emails, texts, and messages we receive daily. We have all learned to "scan" in order to save time. This strategy can help us to be more effective and productive at work and help us to weed through all of things that are thrown our way in a given day.

However, there is a risk to this strategy, isn't there?

Right. Sometimes we're tempted to "scan" something that needs to be read. Out of habit, we speed through something that needs to be "experienced." This could be one of those times. Frankly, you could speed read through this e-book. If you're a "scanner" like me you could get through this content in 20 minutes or less.

But… if you allow yourself to "experience" it… it could take some significant time. Now, the words "significant time" might make you cringe. I assume your life is very full as you juggle multiple roles, duties and tasks. You've probably got things to do at work. You've got things to do at home. In fact, it may be late at night as you read this, and there's a part of you that can't shake the looming thought of the to-do list that is waiting for you.

But… what if you did?

What if you gave yourself some time to think about these questions? What if you really allowed yourself to experience them? What if you found a designated place to think about these ideas and questions? A favorite room in your house? A favorite coffee shop? A favorite park bench? What if you gave yourself permission to take some intentional time to dig in? What could happen?

Could it be time well spent? You bet.

Heck, as you already know this is a big decision. Deciding whether or not to do some kind of coach training is an investment of your time and your cash. More importantly, it's also dedicating yourself to growing a business and breaking through some of the very obstacles that your potential coaching clients will be facing. That's why we call these first five questions the "Critical Questions."

These questions will help you make that decision.

More importantly... if you do decide that coaching is right for you. Now, it's my guess that these questions will light you up! And it's okay if they don't as it just means coaching isn't for you. No hard feelings. You're set free to explore other things. BUT... if these questions get your heart racing (which happens), if they make you grin ear to ear (it's quite possible) and if they fill you with anticipation for an exciting future... that is fantastic too!

So let's do it.

Let's dive in and see where the journey takes you.

Part One: The 5 Critical Questions

Critical Question 1: Are You Willing to Get Paid?

I know that sounds like a crazy question but it's important to ask.

That's right.

Are you willing to get paid?

Now, you might be asking, "Why is it important to ask this NOW?"

Well, we've seen people go through various coach certifications and come out the other side… but they are timid about charging a fee for their services. Sometimes it's just that they've never had to charge a fee for anything other than mowing a lawn or babysitting when they were a kid. So the whole idea of being able to charge $150, $200 or more for an hour of work is something totally new. But for others, it's something deeper.

For some of us, it's a struggle to see that we bring value. It's an internal wrestling match to over-come feelings of doubt and low self worth. As a result, some people are exceedingly uncomfortable with the concept of asking to be compensated for their time.

Maybe you fall within that first camp. It would be

a new habit to ask to be paid generously for your time. Or maybe you're in the second group in which the thought of asking to get paid scares you to your very core. (NOTE: It's okay if you haven't thought about this question! Most people haven't at this point. That's why we're asking the question... now.) But let me ask you again— are you willing to get paid?

If there is any part of you that cringes a little bit at the thought of charging for your time, I want to offer a few thoughts.

You are potentially going to embark on the adventure of getting certified as a life coach. Whether you choose our program or a different one, you're probably going to invest hours and hours of your time to hone your skills, not to mention the dollar investment to develop yourself as a coach.

So you'll be investing in the process.

Now... during that process, you'll be introduced to powerful concepts and strategies that will help you unlock your client's potential. I'm betting you'll practice with other people, and, as you do, you'll bless people's socks off!

That's right. You will bless people's socks off even when you are practicing! Let me give you an example. In our live certifications, we don't role-play. I hate fake scenarios and cheesy set ups. I bet you can identify with that! Instead, we immediately have you apply the coaching strategies that we introduce. Within minutes of being introduced to a coaching concept, you use the strategies to coach another person in the room. It's amazing to see literally breakthrough after breakthrough with people even though it's the first time they have tried a coaching technique.

For example, we recently had a woman who started crying during a practice coaching session. When I saw it, I came over to the pair to check in. The new coach looked a little shocked, like maybe he had done something wrong. But as I knelt down to talk to the woman being coached, I could immediately see that she was crying but smiling at the same time. As those tears kept rolling down her face, she explained that her "coach" had asked her a question that helped her to uncover a belief about herself that had been locking her up for years. She hadn't seen it until that exact point. She explained that once the belief was out in the light, it almost seemed silly. It had been buried. Even though it wasn't something she was really aware of, it was still holding her back and preventing her from taking the steps forward that she needed to take. In fact she said, "That belief was in my blind spot. Now that I'm looking at it, I know it's not true. I can't wait to get started on my business plan now!"

As you can imagine, it was powerful for everyone in the room to see the effectiveness of coaching right in that moment. Plus it made everyone laugh out loud to hear her "coach" let out a sigh of relief and say, "I'm so relieved. I thought I'd broke you! I was ready to blame Mitch because I read that question right out of the book!" It was funny but it was also a great reminder. This new coach was using a concept we had just introduced about 15 minutes prior to them practicing.

Think about it though. If you could coach that kind of breakthrough in that short amount of time, imagine the value you could bring if you had 30 minutes or 30 days to practice it! Seriously… consider the good you could do. Just think about how much you could help someone.

TIP: CHARGE BASED ON VALUE NOT ON TIME

One of the things we challenge people to consider is charging based on the value you bring, not on the amount of time you spend together.

Yes, you can offer tremendous value in a 60-minute coaching session. But, even more importantly, you can bring exponential value to your coaching clients in the periods between your coaching sessions!

For example, I worked with a business attorney to help him find fresh perspective on approaching his practice. I coached him through defining a clear picture of his mission and helped him gain clarity on his passions. In the process, we uncovered that he wanted to make significant shifts to his business model during one of our calls. So, between those calls he implemented some changes, and, within a year, he had almost doubled his income. I was charging him $200 an hour for our sessions, but the changes he implemented were worth well over $100,000.

So again I'll say: Base your price on the potential impact you could have on your client and not on what you think you're worth during that hour of conversation.

Moreover, we find that the fee our clients have to pay helps with their commitment level and accountability. The fee helps people realize that if they are willing to pay for coaching, they are even more committed to making the changes needed to go after the things they want to pursue. So, in a way, the fee you charge helps with the coaching process too.

And here's one last thought on this subject. You may be thinking that you don't want to coach people in businesses. Maybe you want to coach teens on their choices. Or you want to coach teachers on how to balance their work and their lives. Or maybe you want to coach people nearing retirement on how to love the next season of their life. It's okay. The change you help someone make might not affect a $100,000 shift in their business, but let me ask you this. How much is it worth for a parent to have learned how to be fully present with their kids after you coached them on their work-life balance? How much is it worth to the person who moves into retirement with a plan about which they're passionate? How much is it worth for someone to finally realize the work they were created to do and help them build a plan to make it a reality? The word that just keeps coming to mind for me is "priceless." Can I get an amen?

In fact, I can tell you that I've helped people launch products, make more money, get big promotions and achieve dream jobs, and all of those achievements were satisfying. But one of my absolute favorite personal stories from my coaching career came about halfway through a three month (ten session) coaching package with a client. As I was kicking off a call, my client said, "Well this investment in coaching just paid for itself last night." I wasn't sure what she was talking about, so I asked her to clarify. She continued, "Well you know that we've been working on my strategies for work/life balance and really being in the moment with my family." I said, "Absolutely." Then she said, "Well, last night my nine-year-old daughter said that she'd noticed a difference in me. She didn't even know about the coaching I've been doing, but she told me that I seem a lot happier and she just wanted to let me know that she thought that was pretty cool." I said, "Well I think that's pretty cool too!" My client then quietly said, "Yeah, it's very cool. So… Thanks so much for that." Now, I'll tell you that in that particular client's case… she didn't get a big promotion or a big raise. She had made a big investment in coaching, but she didn't see any immediate monetary gain. However, she said that her investment was "priceless." Later, she told me that in hindsight she would have paid double what she paid to get the results she experienced in her life. I quickly joked, "Well my rates just doubled! Shall we start over?" We laughed, but a few months later she referred a co-worker to me. She let them know about my impact AND my new rates. So... yes... When you're talking about coaching and making an impact, "Priceless" is the right word to describe it.

Download the Free AudioBook and Action Guide Journal at: trainingtobealifecoach.com/ action

JOURNALING QUESTIONS

Give it some thought.

Are you willing to get paid? And in many cases… get paid very well?

Here are some journaling questions to ponder around this topic.

What would you do with an extra $2,000 a month or more from coaching?

What if you were able to help someone make a change in their life that they've wanted to make for years? What could that be worth to them?

What would it feel like to make a healthy income while actually helping people do and be more of who they were meant to be?

Critical Question 2: Whom Would You Love To Help?

Seriously, whom do you long to coach?

Is it the person who is struggling with efficiency? Do you continually think of ways to help people organize and set things straight? Does your heart race at the thought of helping them be more productive at work and enjoy being home more, too?

Or do you want to help people get clearer on an idea and launch a business? Do you love the thought of helping someone put together a plan and walking it out? Do you find yourself encouraging innovative ideas and being captured by inspiring entrepreneurial stories?

What if you could help someone (or many someones) to launch new and productive companies?

Or do you find yourself wanting to help people figure out their purpose in life?

Do you naturally ask people about what they love to do? Do you have a passion to help people identify their strengths so they can live them out more often?

I'll give you a personal example.

I was recently asked to come to the corporate offices of a Fortune 100 company to speak to some of their employees about innovation and thinking bigger. While I was sitting in the lobby waiting for my contact, I watched employees walking in and out of the building. I found myself longing to grab each one. I wanted to ask them about their passions and their "sweet spot" in life. I wanted to see if they felt like they were doing what they were called to do. I knew some of them were, but I'm guessing that many of them weren't.

My heart raced as I thought of ways to help each one of them. Yup, those are the types of people I love to work with. Those are my peeps. How about you? Whom do you want to help? Think about it. It's a critical question.

I'll confess that when I first started as a coach, I hadn't spent much time on this. I was passionate about coaching, and I wanted to make an impact, but I didn't get specific. I thought I could help everyone so I tried to reach everyone. You can imagine how well that worked. Whenever I'd talk about coaching, I would describe it with passion, but the "I can help anyone" message didn't really resonate with people. They couldn't really understand what I was doing or whom I was helping so they couldn't connect me with possible clients. Reaching out to friends and people in my network seemed to go nowhere.

I was building my coaching business on the side while working a full time job. Because I didn't

have a focus, I tried to attend every network-
ing event I heard about. After working a full day,
I'd show up at a chamber of commerce gathering looking for clients. Then the next night, I'd
attend a young entrepreneurs club meeting. Then
on Saturday morning, I'd try a class or seminar
to expand my reach and let people know what I
was doing. Without a focal point, it was fruitless
and discouraging.

I have to admit that I was really close to giving up.
I felt like I was already on the ropes and then... I
went to a family gathering and got hit by a sucker
punch that almost knocked my dream of becoming a coach out cold! I was chatting with one of my
uncles and mentioned that I was working on starting my coaching practice. He had some business
experience, so he asked me some questions. Now,
I should also tell you that this is my "grumpy uncle."
(We all seem to have at least one grumpy uncle...
right?) He seems to make it his personal responsibility to shoot down people's ideas and keep them
"safe" by discouraging them from taking risks. Well,
in a weak moment I walked right into his "interroga-
tion tactics" and started to get hit over and over by
questions that I didn't have answers for. Who was
my client? What would they pay? Why would they
need coaching? Why would anyone need coaching?
He just went on and on. He smelled blood and was
relentless. Finally, someone announced dessert
was available, and I escaped and attempted
to recover.

It was tough. I had a dream to help people and to
build a successful business. I was tired of running

and attending meetings that were a bad fit. People didn't seem to know how to help me since I didn't even know what I needed. I didn't want to answer another "how's it going" question, and part of me wanted to chuck it all and stick with the "safe" I already knew.

But then I got some great advice.

A close friend and successful entrepreneur sat me down and began to ask me questions that really helped. He helped me get specific about the kinds of people I was passionate. He asked me about my "ideal" client and with whom I work best. Suddenly, I felt hopeful. I started to feel some passion again. I started to see a light at the end of the tunnel. It wasn't just about helping everyone because when you try to help everyone, you wind up helping no one. Nope, my friend had helped me get focused on whom I could help. This was a huge breakthrough and it made all the difference. How?

Well, once I knew my ideal client... I could talk with a friend about my coaching and relay EXACTLY who my client was in a simple and clear way. As a result, people began referring potential clients to me because they understood with whom I did my best work. I also stopped going to every network-ing event under the sun and only went to the types of events my ideal client would attend. Not only that, but I started to create events that my ideal client would be attracted to. Soon I had created one specific monthly by-invitation-only event that had my ideal client lining up to attend. We even got in the paper due to the response! Before long, the events filled up within minutes of being announced. It was crazy! I loved it because I was able to shape the events with my clients in mind, I was able to have a lot of fun, I was able to grow my business and my impact AND I wound up cutting down the amount of time I was away from my family! Talk about a win-win-win!

Finally, I was even ready for my grumpy uncle. The next time I saw him and he started in with his questions, I was not only able to tell him EXACTLY who I wanted to coach, I could tell him that I was actually coaching them... AND they were paying me! Better yet, they were HAPPY to pay me because we were doing really meaningful work together! (Yeah... that felt really good!)

Now I don't want you to feel like you need to know EVERYTHING about your ideal client. In fact, we will take you through a process in our training that helps you determine that and then build a plan to reach that person... over and over. But for now, I do want you to give yourself permission to dream a little bit about who that ideal client might be for you.

Use these journaling questions as a guide and see where they take you. As you do, know that you'll be head and shoulders above most of the coaches that are trying to build businesses right now. Why? Because most don't ask themselves about this. They are more like I was in the beginning... trying to help EVERYONE, but as a result, reaching NO ONE.

So yeah, dig into these questions and think about YOUR ideal client.

JOURNALING QUESTIONS

Give it some thought. Whom would you love to coach? (Eventually, this kind of thinking will help you get clear on market segments and niches for your coaching practice's business plan. For now, don't worry about that … just dream.) Think about the types of people you could impact and why that's important to you and why it will be important for them. Seriously. Think about this. Before you move on, do the exercise.

By the way… consider this set of questions as a true litmus test on whether or not coaching is for you. How? Well, if you don't want to do the exercise… that's ok. You got your answer on whether coaching is for you. If you want to stop… that's cool. You can stop right now and there are no hard feelings. In fact, I'd say "Well done!" for figuring out that becoming a life coach isn't for you.

But if your heart races at the thought of the people you'll be able to help… If you can't sleep tonight because you're mind is spinning as you think about the people you can impact… if you have a bit of a goofy grin on your face as you even begin to think about working with people that are a perfect fit for you… then groovy. We hit pay dirt. That means becoming a life coach might just be for you! (And to that I say… "woot woot!")

So... let's stay with it.

Describe two to three types of people you would love to coach.

What are some things you would love to help them accomplish, do or change?

What would it feel like to make a healthy income while actually helping people do and be more of who they were meant to be?

Critical Question 3: Are You Willing to SHUT UP?

That's right. I know… I know.

It's a weird but important question to ask.

Are you willing to be quiet?

This is one of the most important questions you need to be asking yourself as you are thinking about becoming a business or life coach.

POWERFUL TOOL

One of the most powerful tools that you'll have as a coach will be the questions you ask. As a coach, you can ask a question that will help your client see a blind spot or a new opportunity in a way they've never seen it before. But the true key to asking a powerful question is being willing to listen.

Now, sadly, we've all probably experienced what it feels like to be asked a question and then not had the chance to answer it. You know how that feels. A friend, a co-worker or a family member asks you a question but instead jumps in to interject their opinion or share their thought on the subject.

Let's be honest. That experience stinks. Even if the information the person offers is valuable, you still feel robbed of the opportunity to answer the question yourself. You might even start to shut down thinking the person really doesn't care about your opinion… or think it matters.

Right?

Conversely, I hope you've experienced someone asking you a question and then sitting back to really listen. They weren't just waiting for their turn to talk again. They really listened to you. They showed you were they were listening with their body language and gave you some prompts from time to time, like a short "Hmmmmm." The person didn't interrupt. They weren't distracted. Or they authentically said something like, "Wow. I hadn't thought of that." Then as you continued, maybe they even took notes! Whew.

What did that feel like?

It felt great… didn't it?

I think we can all agree that in today's fast-paced and distracted world, being listened to is becoming more and more rare. It's becoming revolutionary, in fact. Think about it. When was the last time you REALLY felt listened to? When I ask that question, most people can't remember a recent time. They stop and think about it… but they can't actually remember an example of someone putting down their phone, limiting distractions and fully engaging in what they had to say. It's sad, but we're simply losing our ability to listen.

That's why listening is so important to a coach. When an Elite Life Coach™ combines powerful questions with true listening, it's an incredible experience for the person being coached. They might not even be able to put their finger on why they open up, but as they feel listened to, they will feel honored and empowered. As their Coach engages, reflects and possibly offers a pertinent follow up question... trust will build and they'll begin to open up at deeper levels.

Listening. It's so simple... and so powerful.

So... are you willing to shut up?

If you've gotten this far in the book... I'm betting you're right with me. You're willing to be quiet and truly listen. But... hey... if that's not you... then you can stop reading. You can put this book down and just walk away. Seriously. No harm no foul. You got your answer. Coaching IS NOT for you. Now you know! Now you're set free to pursue other things and that's great! Mission accomplished.

BUT... if you're tracking with this chapter, if you get frustrated when you see people not listening to each other, if you get freakishly frustrated when someone interrupts instead of letting a person finish their thought, if you have a passion for hearing someone out and drawing out their best ideas... then hey... you're right on track. Coaching might just be a part of your DNA. It's a part of who you are and for that... we say... whooohooo!

Stay the course and let's continue.

"One of the most powerful tools that you'll have as a coach will be the questions you ask. But that's not enough. You have to be willing to really listen."– Mitch Matthews

Okay, great. If you're here, it means you have committed to not only asking powerful questions... but you're also all about actively listening to your coaching clients. That's fantastic! I'm excited for you and I'm glad you're "in."

We're going to go a bit deeper now with this "shutting up" question, and where we're headed might surprise you. Why? Well, this is where the question of whether we're really listening as coaches can sneak up on us. Let me explain.

There is no doubt that some coaches bring value by guiding the process and providing innovative strategies and tools. In fact, in our coach training program (The Coach Mindset), we offer loads of specific strategies, effective tools and powerful processes so you can guide your coaching clients through a process of discovery and breakthrough. Imagine the amazing feeling as you guide them on a journey of getting clear on their goals and dreams, putting a plan in place to achieve them and then seeing them take massive action to make those things a reality!

BUT you have to be careful. Some coaches cross the line and go too far. They start to "tell" their clients what to do. They start to direct them too much. Can this make the process faster? You bet. Can it help the person in the short run? Maybe. But if the coaching client is always told what to do... will they really own the solution? Will they value their discoveries if they were too strongly directed toward them?

Maybe. Maybe not.

THE INTELLECTUAL IMMUNE SYSTEM™

I have a theory. I call it the "Intellectual Immune System."

I believe our intellect has an immune system similar to our body's immune system.

Let me explain by painting a picture.

I have a friend who was having significant health problems. After a series of tests, his doctor explained that he needed a new kidney. His mom stepped up to donate one of her kidneys which was a perfect match. They were able to work with one of the best transplant surgeons in the country and the procedure went off without a hitch. So though he knew he needed the transplant, had a perfect match, and the surgery went perfectly…

Even with all of that… what did his body naturally do to the new kidney? It rejected it. Why? Well, because it was foreign. Even though he needed it, his body's immune system saw it as something from outside him and attacked the new kidney.

I believe our intellect does the same thing with ideas. There are a number of studies which prove this, but I'm betting I can rely on your experience. Let me ask you this. Have you ever read a book on seven principles or nine new habits and you fell in love with it? It just felt like a perfect fit and the solution to many of your problems. Maybe it was on leadership, fitness or diet. You loved what the author was saying. It resonated with you. It just felt true. It was almost like they had video cameras up in your office or your home as they were writing it. The solutions just seemed like they were made for YOU!

Did you commit right then and there to start implementing this newfound wisdom? You said, "I'm so doing this!" Or… "This is a solution that I can use!" Or… "This author just gets it. I'm on board with this!"

But then (if you're like me) within a week or two, you'd forgotten principles 4 through 7… or habits 3 through 8? Maybe within four weeks, you'd forgotten the title of the darn book and the author's name? (Can I get an amen?)

Why does this happen?

Well... I'd suggest that it's our Intellectual Immune System (I.I.S.).

Even though a theory or a concept may be a perfect fit, our I.I.S. can kick in and attack it because it's from outside us. On a conscious or subconscious level, we start to say, "Well that's great in theory, but it doesn't fully apply to me." Or "She has a great idea, but it starts to break down when I try it in my world." The deep recesses of our brain push back saying, "The concept is fine but that author has never really walked in MY shoes."

Sound familiar?

I sure know I've experienced this, and from working with hundreds of coaching clients, I've heard about this phenomenon time and time again. It happens to all of us and it gets in the way.

The big question is... "Is there a way around the Intellectual Immune System?" The good news is that the answer is a resounding YES! And it can be wrapped up in one word. That word?...

"Ownership"

That's right. When you coach someone, you help them discover solutions that they OWN. You help them put together a plan that they help to create.

When a coach uses this approach, the solution doesn't come from without, but, rather, from within. As a result… their Intellectual Immune System doesn't attack it. They own it… from start to finish.

That can make all the difference when we're talking about implementing lifelong and life changing solutions. It's also why one-on-one coaching can be more impactful than a weeklong seminar or a best selling book.

Why? Because as Elite Coaches, we help our coaching clients overcome their Intellectual Immune System because…

If they discover it… they own it.

And if they own it, they'll beat their Intellectual Immune System and finally break through!

There is a hidden key to creating ownership and beating the I.I.S. It's subtle, but I'm guessing you already know what I'm going to say. The secret, oftentimes, is being willing to listen. It's being willing to shut up. Effective coaching is all about asking powerful questions and then intentionally listening. It's not always easy to do, but it's revolutionary when you do. Are you willing to shut up? I bet you are. Ask yourself these journaling questions.

JOURNALING QUESTIONS:

Describe an experience from your life
when someone really listened to you.

Who was the person and how did
it help?*

What if you could do that for others on
a consistent basis? What would that
feel like:

*Bonus Suggestion:

What if you let that person who really
listened to you know how much you
appreciated them? Maybe through a
phone call or a note. I'm betting they
would love to hear from you, and they'd
probably be surprised that they had such

an effect on your life! Reach out to say "Thank you so much for listening to me!"

Critical Question 4: Are You Willing To Work Hard?

I know this might seem like a given, but it really is an important question to ask yourself.

Are you willing to work hard?

I know… I know. If we were writing this book as a sales strategy for our coach training program, it would certainly be easier to tell you that becoming a coach is super easy and you'll be making the big bucks in 29 days or less!

But hey! We all know that those are hollow promises. We've all heard them and, although those claims of getting rich quick while not having to work at it are tempting to believe, I know you're a smart cookie. I know you know that anything that's worthwhile is worth fighting for.

Here's the deal.

If you want to become a life coach… there are times when it's just going to be hard. You're going to need to make some sacrifices. For most people, they start by developing their coaching practice on the side. That means coaching a person before or after work or working with someone on a Saturday morning.

That's how I got started.

I was working a full-time sales position, but it wasn't satisfying, and it wasn't where I wanted to be long term. However, it paid the bills and I wanted to do a good job for the company for whom I was working. So I went through coach certification on my own time and on my own dime. Then I came back home to the Midwest and began to coach people on the east and west coasts. I used the time zones to my advantage. At 7 am (central), I could coach someone on the east coast before I went to work. Since it's 8 am for them it worked well. Then on other days, I would work with someone on the west coast later in the day. I could call them after 5 pm my time, and it would still be during their workday.

That schedule may sound strenuous, but it paid off. I was able to bring in a lot of extra cash that helped my family build our reserves for our launch into coaching, speaking and consulting full time.

Yes, it made for some long days, but it was a true springboard into what I dreamed of doing. Plus, it was exciting for my family. My boys were young, and I would talk with them about this dream and why I was working so hard. They got inspired and it became a part of their DNA, too. Just as a side note: I've been a full-time entrepreneur for 12+ years, and our sons have watched this transformation. They've seen the hard work and they've also seen how it has paid off. They don't look at a "job" in the same way their friends do. They are constantly looking for entrepreneurial approaches to making money since that's what they've seen. In fact, I knew we had really made our kids "weird" in all the right ways when our youngest son opened a lemonade stand on a hot summer day. When most kids would make $10 or $25 over the course of a few hours, our son made over $300 in a couple of hours because he'd learned to approach it like an entrepreneur! Did it take a little extra effort to set up on the front end? You bet. Was he working hard while he was out in that July heat? Yes! But the sweaty smile on his face was priceless after he was done. And that's the kind of satisfaction you'll feel too. Will you have to work hard? I promise you... you will need to. BUT... there's just something different about working hard for...

- Something you believe in!
- Something that blesses your clients' socks off!
- Something which blesses you too!

Now, again, there may be coach training programs and certifications that promise you it will be easy. But it won't be. It takes hard work to build a coaching practice. I bet you know that. And honestly, I'd be cautious of anyone who would tell you otherwise. At the same time, I'll admit that sometimes it almost breaks my brain because, as a coach, I get paid very well to help people I really enjoy working with achieve the life they've always wanted. Now that is what I call a true win-win situation!

It takes intentionality. It takes determination. It

takes work.

And it will be some of the most rewarding work you will ever do! There are nights that my head hits the pillow and I have a big goofy grin on my face as I think back through some of the day's coaching sessions. Maybe I asked the right question that enabled someone to rediscover a big dream that had gotten buried along the way. Maybe I helped someone push through a belief that was holding them back. Maybe I celebrated as someone finally took action and made progress toward a lifelong goal that had eluded them. It's hard work, but it's so worthwhile.

I'll also tell you that our graduates have coaching packages that range from $1,500 to $20,000. It's hard work that can be very lucrative! In fact, the national average for a business coach fee is $150 an hour. Again, are you willing to work hard? I bet you are. Let's dig into a few journaling questions on the subject.

JOURNALING QUESTIONS:

What will be some of the rewards of doing the hard work of setting up my own coaching practice?

What will it feel like to have a thriving coaching practice?

Describe some reasons why it may be important to get started now.

Critical Question 5: Are You Willing To Take The Biggest Risk?

Okay… as we're wrapping up our 5 Critical questions, I have a final question for you.

It might be the most important question you ask yourself. It's critical to establishing trust with your clients, and it's key to not only enjoying being a coach but also thriving as a coach. It's a question most people won't ask you because they're scared to. And don't worry, it's not a sales pitch.

It's just one more question that I wish someone had asked me before I started being a coach.

Are you willing to be yourself?

That's right. It's a critical question to ask. Why? Because there is a temptation that hits when people start the process of becoming a coach. It's tempting to try to appear perfect. I know it hit me hard when I was first getting started.

For example, initially I wanted to coach people to be more successful. So, I thought, "I need to be successful." Okay, I'll admit that this probably happened more at a subconscious level but it was there. That thought in and of itself isn't terrible, but the temptation to appear perfect started to slip in. It wasn't so much that I needed/wanted to be successful, it was that I kept pushing myself to LOOK successful. It impacted everything. I slowly started to dress differently because I was trying to "look" successful. I went from wearing my favorite fleece pullovers and jeans to wearing sports coats and expensive shirts. Now, sports coats and expensive shirts aren't bad. In fact, I still like to wear them from time to time. But at that time, I was wearing them because I thought that's what I needed to wear. I started to stretch myself thin because I pushed myself to attend a lot of events that I thought successful people would attend. They weren't necessarily events I wanted to attend, but they were the things I thought I had to be seen at in order to look "successful." Once there, I'd be tempted to try to act "successful." I wouldn't really be my authentic self, I would just try to be what I thought I needed to be in that moment. It almost sounds laughable as I write this, but I'm guessing you've been tempted to try to be something you're not… in order to fit in.

That was where I was and, as you can imagine, it was exhausting! It was really difficult to connect with people on a deeper level because I was trying to maintain a persona in these situations. So here I was… wanting to be the safe place for people and help them feel comfortable, but I wasn't even comfortable in my own skin. Ironic? Maybe. Tragic? Sure. Common? You bet!

The key is to be YOU!

When you are authentically YOU... imperfections and all... it makes it so much easier to establish trust. AND it makes it a whole lot more fun!

When you're not, when you're tempted to try to appear that you have it all together and have it all worked out, it can be brutal. It hurts your ability to establish trust, rapport and true connection with your clients. And these are critical if you want to make a significant impact with your ally.

I'm happy to say that over time I was able to shake this temptation to try to be something I'm not. I was just able to settle in and be me. It was completely freeing and it had a HUGE impact on my coaching. I'm wildly blessed to say that the connection and the trust I have with clients is amazing because I can be open, honest and transparent with them. In fact, I've even had clients tell me that because I am transparent with them, they feel released to be transparent with me!

I'll never forget the time I was working with one of my highest tiered clients. He had paid five figures for his coaching package and was a C.E.O. of an impressive organization. At one point he asked me a question about a specific approach to a situation. I'd never been asked the question before so I didn't have an immediate answer. That temptation to be perfect raised its ugly head for a nano-second and I thought about trying to fake my way through an answer. But I got hold of myself and remembered who I was. After a few seconds of silence, I said, "I don't know the answer to that, but let's figure out an answer together." There were a few more seconds of silence and then he said, "Wow! I'm soooooo using that response. I like that a lot!" He continued, "There are so many times that I'm scared someone is going to ask me a question I don't know the answer to, but I'm going to use that. Yes, I do like that."

So I didn't have THE answer, but I had an answer that allowed me to stay authentically me, help my client and move our relationship forward. That's what can happen when you give yourself the permission to be authentically you. And as you do, you'll give your clients that ability to be more true to themselves too!

So, consider this...

Are you willing to be you... the best you... but YOU all the same?

I bet you are! Again, just to hit it home, I'll leave you with a few journaling questions.

JOURNALING QUESTIONS:

Describe someone from your life who is/ was authentic and genuine.

Now, think about how that impacted your relationship with that person. Did it increase or decrease level of trust and connection? Describe how it helped you to connect with that person?*

Describe how you think this approach of being authentic would impact your ability to coach people.

How will it feel to be your authentic self as you coach others?

CONGRATULATIONS!

Okay, congratulations! You've completed the first 5 Critical Questions.

How do you feel?

More importantly, how are you feeling about becoming an Elite Life Coach? If we were in elementary school, I might send you a note that has a "Yes" box and a "No" box under the question: "Do you want to be a coach?"

Which would you check?

Did the first five questions make you think twice about whether coaching is for you? Did they make you want to run in the other direction? or did they reinforce that you really connect with coaching?

If you're reading this, then I'm betting it was the latter.

Heck… if you're like some of the people who make it through these first five important questions, you have the feeling of…

"Coaching is the thing I've always wanted to do."

Or maybe…

"It's what I do naturally… I've just not known what to call it!"

If that's you, then great! I'm betting that nothing can stop you at this point.

Actually, I'm hoping that's the case! There's a tremendous need for great coaches.

There are countless people who need people like you to help them:

- get clear on what they want to do and be
- get "unstuck"
- draw up a plan that they can own and walk out
- start making the changes they need to make
- achieve the life they were created to live!

So if you're feeling the "call" to be a coach, if you have a passion for helping people in this way… you're on the right path.

Now, we're on to the next set of questions.

You might be saying, "Wait. What? I thought I was 'in'."

Yes, if you're this far into the book, you've proven

you have a heart for coaching. You've also got passion and drive. I'm guessing you also have some natural gifting that will help you be an incredible coach. That's something to celebrate!

This additional set of questions will simply help you take the next critical step in this journey.

These are questions designed by my good friend and business partner, David Nadler.

David is a lifelong entrepreneur. No kidding. He ran his first business (a sign building company) when he was only 13 and his first client was a small city. In fact, he made the pitch to the Mayor and closed the deal all by himself! He's run brick and mortar businesses, he's been a successful consultant and he's had tremendous success as an online marketer.

Back in 2010, he decided to attend the LIVE version of the Coach Mindset—Elite Life Coach Training and Certification. Before he had even completed the training, David had secured a $2,000 client! He's been coaching business owners and entrepreneurs ever since. He just knows how to build successful and sustainable businesses.

So much so that a few years ago he came to me to say that he wanted to help me take the Coach Mindset online. I was resistant at first because I LOVED delivering the training LIVE, and I didn't want to compromise the quality of the training in any way. However, he showed me the different advances in technology and some of the remarkable things we could deliver via an online format. Then we walked out the process together, and, in a very short time we've been able train thousands of coaches from around the world! It's been an amazing journey, and I'm wildly blessed to have been working with David.

As we discussed this book, I talked about these first five questions and how important they were to helping me and many other people decide that coaching was the right fit. As David and I discussed these, he raised a great point. He said that people who investigate coaching first need to figure out whether it's right for them. Once they've established that, their confidence starts to grow. BUT then they have another set of doubts that often creep in. These almost always center on the question of whether they can actually make coaching into a business. They're excited about the idea of coaching, but since many have never actually run their own business, they question whether they can really have a successful and sustainable coaching practice.

I challenged him to go further with this and prepare this next set of five questions. These focus on the business-building side of coaching. I'll tell you straight up…these questions will challenge you and they'll stretch you. They're the very questions most coaching schools NEVER want you to think about before signing up for a program. Why? Because they don't want you to think about the "real world" aspects of coaching as a career. That's where we're a little different. You might even call us "weird." We want you to go into this decision with your eyes wide open! We want you to be confident in your decision and aware of some of the challenges and opportunities that exist within the economics and business-side of the coaching world. (That's also why over half of the content in our program actually deals with the business of coaching!)

Get ready but also get excited.

I know when I was first investigating coaching, I hadn't really sold my own services since I mowed lawns as a 12 year old. I didn't come from a long line of entrepreneurs. Heck my dad was the warden in a prison and my mom was an accountant! They were AMAZING parents but we didn't have a lot of entrepreneurial conversations at our house. As a result, I really wondered whether I'd have the chops to do it. I struggled with not knowing what I didn't know. I wondered what was in my blind spot. I doubted myself, mostly because I didn't know what it would take.

That's exactly why we included this next set of questions. They will help you to get a better understanding on whether coaching… and more specifically… whether building a coaching business is for you.

If not… that's okay. At least you know. You can go and do something else and not waste a second more of your time on this. BUT… if you get through these next five questions… and you come out the other side excited about coaching… then anything is possible! You'll be able to move forward with incredible confidence and awareness. You'll be empowered to move past any feelings of being "stuck" and be able to take action to make your dream of being a successful life coach a reality!

So dig in and see where the questions take you!

Part Two: The 5 Critical Business Questions

Question 1: Can you be an expert?

In today's age the word "expert" gets thrown around a lot. It's kind of like the words "award winning" or "world famous." A lot of people use the words, but we rarely stop to think about what they actually mean. And frankly, in most situations, words like this mean very little! As we begin to move toward becoming a solo-preneur, an entrepreneur engaged in a one-person business, we need to dig deep and look at how we define "expert".

Even if we've never stopped to consider the definition of "expert", we DO define it within ourselves. We ascribe expert status to those around us, and possibly ourselves.

If I ask you to tell me what an expert is, you'd likely tell me that it is someone who has authority on a subject. Probably someone who has studied the topic in depth—perhaps for the greater part of their life. I often hear that it is someone who has practiced extensively in their area and achieved at least some success in implementing whatever it is they are an expert on. These are good definitions.

There is a problem, however, with this picture as a definition of "expert".

The problem is that these definitions come from the head. To tackle critical question number one, we have to look beyond head definitions and get down to the deeper level.

So let me ask you to do something for me. Instead of asking you to define what an expert is, I want to ask you to give me a picture of an expert. Close your eyes for a just a minute and ask yourself, "Whom do I know who is an expert?"

What did you come up with?

Chances are, you have a picture of someone who has devoted years to their trade or industry. Our pictures are full of people like the 30 year tenured professor who has spent her entire life devoted to the study of botany. Or perhaps the 50 year old marketing veteran who has worked in countless companies, large and small, and has been studying and implementing marketing strategies for decades. For myself, the picture that comes to mind is my father who became a Jesus follower at 21 years old and spent the next 35 years of his life devoted to learning those texts that illuminate his faith and teaching them to others.

We have powerful images of what it means to be an expert. And in these powerful images lies the problem.

The Problem with Our Definitions of Experts

The problem with defining an expert as someone who has 10, 20 or 30 years experience in a field is significant. When most of our pictures of experts conjure thoughts of people who have painstakingly devoted their lives to a singular academic or industry pursuit, it starts to color and slant our view of what it takes to become an expert.

It is a serious problem because it sets an unmotivating and unrealistic timeline for our own work toward mastery (a term that I will use to describe the skill sets of an expert).

Some of us are working hard to become experts in our field, but the idea of waiting for decades to achieve it is not very motivating. And it's not helpful in the process of building a business.

Here's why.

Most people can become an expert in a field in as few as three to six months.

What?!? Really?!? Am I off my rocker?

I don't think so. I think that most people, when truly motivated and ready to invest what is necessary, can become an expert in a field in less than a year.

To do so, however, we have to alter our view of what an expert is. I'm not suggesting that we stop viewing 30 year veterans in a field as experts, but rather, I am suggesting that it's necessary to also include another picture of experts into our thinking.

THE 80/20 RULE FOR EXPERTS

To illustrate my point, I'll refer to the 80/20 principle, originally credited to Vilfredo Pareto under the name "The Pareto Principle" and more recently expounded on by Richard Koch, author of "The 80/20 Principle."

I'll quickly break down the principle for you, though it is a fascinating subject to study in depth (I consider myself an expert on the topic):

The 80/20 rule, or the Pareto Principle simply states that for many events, 80% of the effects come from 20% of the causes.

Pareto famously discovered this in his field of study by noting that 80% of the land in Italy was owned by 20% of the people and that 80% of the peas in his garden were produced by 20% of the pea pods.

Recently, this rule has been found to be accurate in hundreds of other areas. Organizations often note that 80% of their sales come from 20% of their customers. People routinely work to discover the 20% of their work "inputs" that produce 80% of the desired outcomes.

How does this apply to being an expert?

Well . . . pretty simply. The 80/20 Rule suggests that 80% of the people in any discipline (biking, coaching, growing tomatoes, business, etc) are beginners.

Think about that for a second. How many people do you know who have taken piano lessons? How many of them are still considered beginners?

In any field of study, somewhere around 80% of the people participating are relatively new to the discipline.

What this means is that in order to be an expert, we don't need to be better than every other person in our field. We just need to be better than 80%! And being more knowledgeable, more skillful, and more educated than 80% isn't nearly as difficult to achieve.

Let's further the example using a coach-business specific.

In order to set yourself apart as a coach, do you need to be the most educated person around on coaching? Not at all. You just need to know more than 80% of the general public in coaching.

To build a successful coaching business, do you need to know more about marketing your coaching practice than everyone else? No. To set yourself apart, you just need to know more than 80% of others out there doing the same thing.

This mental shift in the definition of an expert makes a significant impact on how we approach becoming coaches and solo-preneurs. We no longer have the burden of becoming one of the most educated coaches in the United States (although there is nothing wrong with that goal—it is a worthy pursuit).

Do you see how this definition of expert frees us up to be more of who we were created to be? How it empowers us to go after our dreams to help people as coaches? It helps us throw off one of the most stifling mental barriers to coaching—that is, the belief that we need to study it for years and years and years and know everything there is to know in order to be effective!

LETTING GO, AND BEING AN EXPERT

When I am willing to let go of my deep pictures of "expert" represented by the 30 year veteran, I'm freed up to make something happen. I'm free to move into new pursuits CONFIDENT that I can give coaching a solid study and begin to help people as an expert without spending years developing that expert status.

When I worked at a radio station, I developed expert status in radio in a few years.

When I started a cognitive skills training center, I developed expert status on brain function in a matter of months.

When I started to coach, I developed expert status in a few months.

Throughout all these endeavors, I have developed expert status in many other things, including marketing, communications, team leadership and a host of others.

Does that mean I don't think I have anything to learn in these areas? No.

Does it mean I think I can't learn from people who have expert status in these areas, too? Definitely not!

Does it mean that I don't have a high degree of respect for people who have devoted even more time than I to their field of study? Most certainly not!

But I am an expert in all these things. I may not speak at national conventions on all these topics (although I have), but I can effectively use my expert status to help people in these areas— especially the 80% of those people who are relative beginners!

80% IN MY LIFE

I want to give you a couple examples of how using the 80/20 rule in my life has opened up new opportunities, helped me give myself permission to dream, and to even achieve some things that have been pretty fun for me.

When I first went through The Coach Mindset, I had the same fears and concerns as most other people. Things like "will I be any good at this?" . . . and "can I really justify charging $100 or $200 an hour for my time?" There was a part of me that wanted to continue to study. Part of me wanted to continue to practice and practice until I felt my coaching skills were just right. Part of me even wondered if I should go through another certification process just to make sure I hadn't missed anything.

But there was another part of me that recognized, "Hey, I think I'm going to be good at this." I talked myself through it and was able to give myself the permission to just move forward one step at a time. I was able to reason with myself and tell myself:

1) you have a natural gift for this (in some ways, I'd been coaching all my life)

2) you have invested in yourself and gotten good, solid training that will serve you and your clients well and

3) you know what you need to know to get started!

I was informally working with a couple of people,

kind of coaching-consulting. I was receiving calls here and there as people wanted to "pick my brain" about business. And then the fateful moment came when one of those people said, "I just feel so good when I talk to you, I feel like it's so helpful, you should do this as a business." Perhaps I paused longer than I should have (as I worked up the courage), but my next words were something like, "Well, as a matter of fact, I have just gone through a process to learn the tools and strategies I need to be able to help people professionally as a coach. If you're interested, I'd like to take you through that process and see if it might be a good fit."

And BAM—I was off. I closed that client and two others in the next couple of weeks.

I wasn't 100% confident. I still got a bit of a cold sweat before my first call wondering if I could deliver—wondering if I had the goods. But I took the first step and pushed into that bit of unknown. I trusted that I had 80% of what I needed that would allow me to help 80% of people. And it worked! There's no telling where I would be right now if I hadn't given myself permission to BE the expert that I already was.

So . . . It's time for YOU to let go of your picture of what it means to be an expert, and adopt a view that will allow you to become an expert coach and solo-preneur in less time than you ever thought possible.

Are you willing to be an expert? I'm guessing so. In

fact, it's probably one of the reasons you're burning to help people as a coach. Spend a few minutes on these journaling questions, and see where they take you!

Download the Free AudioBook and Action Guide Journal at: trainingtobealifecoach.com/action

JOURNALING QUESTIONS:

What message do you long to share with people? What's the "first draft" of the vision or story you feel compelled to share with the world? You may already have people seeking your opinion or help on this!

What do you need to do to get to 80%? What training, experience or learning might you need to look at right now to become an expert in the next few months as a coach?

In what categories have you been thinking of being an expert? (things like coaching, marketing, accounting, etc.) In what categories do you feel you really need to be an expert, and what things might it make sense to let go of right now?

Bonus Questions:

What could the next 3-6 months look like if you dedicated yourself to becoming an "80% Expert" in life or business coaching?

What might life look like this time next year if you committed yourself to becoming an expert?

Question 2: Are you willing to wear lots of hats?

This is one of the questions that so many first time entrepreneurs forget to ask themselves.

First, let me tell you a quick story about my time as a brain trainer, and then we'll get back to the question.

THE TYPICAL STORY

My most recently concluded entrepreneurial story is that I started and managed two LearningRx franchise locations in my hometown of Des Moines, Iowa. LearningRx is a company that helps students learn and read faster and easier by increasing their cognitive capacity. Super fun stuff to be involved in and a great company.

When we started our first franchise, my hope and goal was to be the fastest LearningRx startup in the history of the company and to set new records for revenue generation.

After our first 18 months in business, we had accomplished the first goal, and were on our way to achieving the second. We won enough awards in our first year there that it became something of a joke in the LearningRx community. Well, because of that and because I wore loud paisley pants up on stage to accept the awards!

Having this success was awesome for us, and a real tribute to the team we had in place. It was an exhilarating and busy time. As we started to get recognition for our success, both inside the LearningRx system and outside it, something interesting happened.

I started to get more phone calls.

Perhaps you know the kind I'm talking about. They start with a "Hi David . . . " And shortly build to a "I was wondering if I could pick your brain. . . "

Now, if you've not had this happen to you YET, I can tell you that it's pretty cool. An ego boost no doubt.

But people consistently asked me one question that got on my nerves (because I didn't have a good answer for them).

They asked, "what does a typical day look like for you?"

Typical day? I really had no idea how to answer. And at first, not having an answer made me kind of insecure. It made me think that perhaps my success had been a fluke. That perhaps it wasn't based on any skill of mine or the dedication of my team . . . but just a happy accident. At some point it occurred to me that I didn't need to be embarrassed that I didn't really have a solid answer to that question. Why not? Well, because I wore a TON of hats.

I wore the marketing hat. I wore the accounting hat. I wore the trainer and recruiter and vacuumer hat. I wore the stay up late thinking about how to drive more client satisfaction hat. I wore the "run-to-the-bank" hat, the "we-have-a-frustrated-customer" hat and "a-student-just-threw-up-in-the-lobby" hat. I wore so many hats that I'd have a tough time even remembering them all!

At the time, I thought this was a weakness. I wanted to be able to tell people that I sat around being strategic all day. The truth was that strategic thinking (as a strict discipline) was lucky to get a few hours of my week. But that didn't mean I wasn't being a good entrepreneur. In fact, I think that embracing all the hats that I wore—and learning to love it—was one of the defining pieces of our success.

EMBRACING THE HATS

Every entrepreneur has to wear a lot of hats. It's unavoidable.

It's one of the wonderful, difficult, exhilarating and terrifying truths about starting a new business venture!

I've coached a lot of entrepreneurs and solo-preneurs and there is one type of entrepreneur that makes my skin crawl just a little bit. The conversation with them goes something like this.

Coach: So what are a few things going on in your

business that you'd like to consider focusing on for the next 3 months or so?

Ally: Well, I really love my business. I love doing what I do. The problem is that I have to spend all this time working on marketing, selling, financials, administration and all that stuff! I just want you to help me get a system in place so that I don't need to think about all that stuff. Then I can focus on my job.

Coach: . . .

Coach: . . .

Coach: . . .

Coach: All that stuff IS your job! You don't want to be an entrepreneur! You want to have a job!

I'm not at all saying that in order to be a success-ful coach or entrepreneur you have to instantly become an expert in all areas of business. Great leaders know that they need good people on their team who can do the things that they cannot or do not want to do.

But you do need to be able and willing to embrace wearing lots of hats!

Wearing all these hats is one of the primary reasons that I LOVE being a coach. When I get up in the morning, I never hate my job. Most often, I wake up excited about how I get to go to work doing something I love. There is a real exhilaration in being in control. If I have a good idea when I'm running in the morning, I can often start implementing it in the afternoon. Wearing that hat is about as good as it gets.

Also, I really enjoy being able to have some control over what hats I wear . . . and what hats I give to other people. One hat I don't love to wear, for example, is the accounting hat. I mean, I'm ok at accounting . . . in that I understand numbers ok, but if I had to manage debits and credits, my business would be in a world of hurt–so I ask my accountant to wear that hat. And my businesses require lots of presence on the web. I'm decent at thinking through websites and building content, but I don't do HTML. That's a hat I've given to my web developer.

There is something uniquely satisfying about wearing all these hats, and having the responsibility be on me, and me alone. It doesn't mean that I do all jobs, but it does mean that I get to decide what I do, how I do it, and when I do it. That is a freedom that I'm in love with!

So . . .

How about you?

Are you willing to wear a lot of hats? Are you excited about the idea of doing different things every day to make your coaching business work? Do you love the idea of making the decisions in your life and business to grow, stretch and challenge yourself? If so, check out the journaling questions below to get even more definition on that desire!

JOURNALING QUESTIONS:

Describe what it would feel like to have a higher level of variety in your daily life?

What are some of the hats that you're excited to wear as you get started as a life or business coach?

As you think about some of the hats you might need to wear as you grow your business, which seem to be holding you back? How could you look at these differently? And/or whom could you enlist to help you in these areas?

Question 3: Are you willing to be an entrepreneur?

After talking about all the hats an entrepreneur wears, this might seem like a bit of a crazy question. Though you're excited about the variety that you're going to experience in your day as a life or business coach, there's another aspect of being an entrepreneur that I want to call out. One that we really need to be aware of as we're starting any new venture. In fact, this one isn't specific to entrepreneurs, it affects everyone. It has, however, a special effect on people who are working for themselves.

I have a theory about people. I believe we all have two different sides to our personality and need to recognize and be ready for how it will affect us as business owners.

I call my theory . . . Boxers and Whippets.

BOXERS AND WHIPPETS

Let me tell you a quick story that will show you the two entrepreneurs I believe all of us have inside.

When I was young, I had a friend with the coolest dog. I had never heard of this kind of dog before, but my friend Mike started bragging him up before he even got him.

"He's a Whippet," he said.

Apparently this was supposed to be self explanatory. It was not.

Further conversation exposed the fact that Whippets are bred from greyhounds and, though smaller, are nearly as fast. They are the fastest accelerating dogs in the world.

So ok, I'm intrigued, and I'm ready to see this dog in action. Head over to Mike's house and he pulls out one of those long-handled tennis ball launchers. It works great because Mike lives on a big lot and has tons of room for this dog to run.

Mike fires away and the dog is off like a shot. It was truly amazing. Incredible speed and amazing energy.

We threw that ball over and over.

And over and over.

The dog loved to run as much as we loved to watch it.

The only problem came when the dog collapsed on the ground next to Mike, thoroughly exhausted (but completely unharmed). If that dog would have had one more lap in him, he would have given it to us. He was bred to run, and that's exactly what he did.

Ran until he could run no more. He collapsed happy and satisfied!

Now, I have some experience with dogs. Being from a hunting family, we've had bird dogs around for as long as I can remember. But when my wife and I got married, we wanted a different kind of dog. I was doing some research and ran across the most beautiful dog I have ever seen. It was a Boxer. Ever seen one? They truly are magnificent!

We went through the whole process to get a papered Boxer. . . and he was regal. Absolutely magnificent. People would literally drive by my house and talk to my dog. One guy used to roll down his window and yell, "Fine looking dog. Fine looking dog!" I was in love.

You might be able to see where this story is going.

After a few weeks, I decided it was time to get this dog trained up properly. Having experience only with dogs bred to be retrievers, I decided that a quick and fun game of fetch was in order. Armed with a small pile of treats for positive reinforcement, I set out into the back yard with Caesar in tow (isn't that a great name for a boxer?!?).

Properly prepared, I launched the ball. Not too far, just a short throw, and Caesar knew what to do. Not as fast as a Whippet, but he gathered up the tennis ball with decent speed and rightly brought it back to me. So far, so good.

I praised him lavishly and gave him a treat.

And I threw the ball again.

Caesar looked at me. Then at the ball. Then slowly proceeded to trot over to the ball where he looked at me inquisitively. With some encouragement, he picked it up and returned it to me again.

More praise. More treats.

I threw the ball again.

Caesar looked at me like I was crazy.

I cannot know for sure, but his look said something like, "If you want the darn ball, you're going to have to stop throwing it."

No amount of coaching, coaxing or cajoling could turn Caesar into a running, retrieving dog. He was bred to be a guard dog. In fact, boxers were bred in Germany and are often used as guard dogs, military dogs and search and rescue aids. They are fiercely loyal to their families and extremely independent . . . both GREAT qualities.

So why do I tell this story about two dogs? Well, I'm pretty convinced that we all have a little bit of Boxer and Whippet in us.

- The Whippet in us can get up early and run till we collapse.
- The Boxer knows what is important and will do whatever it takes to protect the people it loves.
- The Whippet has a singular focus and goes after it with everything it has.
- The Boxer in us can be pretty laid back and values loyalty over silly games.
- The Whippet runs full out and crushes the competition.
- The Boxer in us can relax and spend time with family and friends . . . or take a nap, and look great doing it.

We all have these two sides in our personality, and they come out even more obviously when we work for ourselves. In a typical "employee" situation, these parts of our personalities are often repressed. We are motivated by typical "carrot and stick" approaches. We get praised when we do our work well, and we get reprimanded when we don't.

But when you're an entrepreneur . . . No one else has a carrot. Or a stick.

No one wakes you up in the morning to tell you to go to work. You also don't hear a whistle at the end of the day to tell you to go home and be with your family.

You have to balance within yourself the two sides

of the equation. You have to be careful of being too driven, or not driven enough. Too much drive and you risk burnout, relational problems and potential health concerns. Too little drive and you risk seeing the end of your entrepreneurship journey. To go back to my Boxer and Whippet story—you need to learn how to be a Whixer :)

We're going to need to be able to draw clear boundaries for ourselves. When do we need to go after things with the tenacity of a Whippet? When do we need to learn to relax, enjoy life, and protect the people and things that are most valuable to us like a Boxer?

I know there are some days when the Whippet in me drives me to perform in ways that I would never be able to if I didn't respect him and let him off his leash. I even have specific ways (rituals you might call them) for drawing him out and getting him worked up! There are also days when I have to nurture the Boxer in me. The Boxer tells me to guard my family and my friends. The Boxer tells me that if I don't take time to hang out on the boat with my family mid-week, if I don't listen to the Boxer when he tells me to take a long bike ride on a Tuesday morning, then all the work that the Whippet is doing will quickly become pointless.

So, are you ready to be an entrepreneur? As you think about this question, think about the Boxer and the Whippet inside. Think about the freedom that you want to have as you start your life and business coaching career. Time freedom, money freedom and people freedom are all waiting for you . . . No matter what kind of dog you may be.

JOURNALING QUESTIONS:

What are some of the things you look forward to about working for yourself either part time or full time?

What resonated with you about the Boxer vs Whippet story? Which personality do you most identify with? How do you think that will be a strength for you as you become a life or business coach?

What pitfalls do you think you'll want to be aware of as you become more of an entrepreneur?

What do you get excited about when you think about working for yourself?

Question 4: Do you have 15 minutes to spare?

This question might seem really obvious. I mean, of course you're going to have to devote time to becoming a coach and building your practice, right?

Well, yes, but I've found that our culture has put forward a vision of "starting a business" that isn't tremendously helpful (or effective, based on my observations).

In addition, one of the questions I get asked a lot as a coach and a coach trainer is "how long will it take me to build my business to the point where I can quit my job?"

In order to answer that question, I want to introduce you to "the compounding effect of time" and ask you "do you have 15 minutes to spare?"

THE COMPOUNDING EFFECT OF TIME & LEARNING

We've all seen the graphs. You're talking to an investment advisor, or perhaps fiddling with an online app, trying to figure out how much to save for retirement.

You plug your numbers in and see an upward curve that's . . . Not quite as upward as you hoped it'd be.

You're thinking that you can't really save any more right now, but you're tempted by the thought "what if I had started this ten years ago?"

You start over and enter an age ten years prior, and the upward curve shoots off the screen. Your stomach drops as you realize that if you'd just started saving a few bucks a week when you were a fetus, you'd be set for life!

Why am I talking about compounding interest? I believe that time and education work the same way.

When you invest 15 minutes in your education and business NOW, it is worth some amount MORE than 15 minutes invested in the future.

If I begin learning to start and run a business for 15 minutes today, it is worth more than that same amount invested in the future because I get to use that knowledge starting IMMEDIATELY.

Most of us aren't ready to make the leap to full time entrepreneurship today. We have families. We have mortgages. We may even have jobs that we like reasonably well. We want to have an avenue where we can have a massive positive impact on other people and make good money doing it, but we're not necessarily in a position to quit our jobs just yet. At least not until our new business proves its ability to support us financially.

There are actually a lot of reasons to start

out slowly.

The compounding effect of time and learning is one of the biggies. The compounded investment of 15 minutes a day learning something new is immensely more impactful than spending the same amount of time learning it all at once at some point in the future.

Getting started now, in a smaller and more manageable way, instead of putting off your learning till a future date will:

- Compound the value of your learning!
- Give you something consistent and predictable to work with!
- Make you more likely to stick with it!
- Allow you to enjoy the journey!
- Limit your stress because it limits your risk!

No one can really answer the question "how long will it take me to turn coaching into a full time job." I scored three clients within 30 days of becoming a coach. That was good for me. Not enough to live on, but $8,000 in 30 days was pretty good for me at that time.

Some coaches need more ramp up time. Some need less. Some coaches can devote lots of time and resources to getting started. Some have more restrictions to work around, both in terms of time and money.

But let's get back to our original question, "Do you have 15 minutes to spare?"

THE VALUE OF 15 MINUTES

If you're still reading this book, then you're probably able to devote 15 minutes a day to developing your coaching skills and your coaching business. In fact, you've already invested that for today by reading this book!

Let's look at what 15 minutes a day looks like.

- **15 minutes a day is 91 hours a year.** What do you think you could accomplish if you took two full weeks to pursue your coaching dreams?
- **30 minutes a day is 182 hours per year.** That's 22 full work days. Most people work about 166 hours per month at a full time job. 30 minutes a day is like having over a month of work time!
- **60 minutes a day is 365 hours per year.** Do you think you could become an expert coach if I gave you over two full time months to get it done? I know you can. I've done it and I've seen others do it too!

So remember this as you consider this journey. As

you become more and more sure that coaching is for you and that you want to have an amazing impact on the people you coach and make a great living as you do, you don't HAVE to jump into it full time! At least not at first. In fact, because of the compounding value of time and education, I actually recommend that you don't. The value of learning over a period of time is amazingly powerful, and it limits risk in ways that I've really grown accustomed to. The last three businesses that I've started, I've developed in this way. First, by giving it a few hours a week. Then a day a week. Then more. By the time I'm ready to go "full time," I have a base of knowledge, skill and experience on which to build. I also have income already waiting for me in my new ventures!

If this concept is resonating with you, check out the following journaling questions to help you define your "15 Minutes!"

Journaling Questions

What amount of time do you feel you can invest in becoming a coach right now? Do you have 15 minutes a day? 30? 60 or more?

What might you consider cutting from your daily or weekly "tIme budget" to add to the value of your investment? For example, could you cut back on time spent watching TV? Are there other things you're willing to forgo to maximize your investment right now?

What excited you about the concept of the compounding effect of time and learning?

Question 5: What will you do with an extra $2,000 each month?

This is one of my favorite questions for sure!

I've never started a business JUST for the money, but I'll be honest, if it weren't for the financial opportunity (along with getting to work for myself, wear lots of different hats and having tons of time and people freedom), I probably wouldn't still be starting businesses!

Most coaches resonate with the idea of helping people and sharing a message. You could probably also put $2,000 a month to good use . . . And that's what this question is all about! Most coaches charge $150 to $200 an hour, and typically coaching packages are sold in 10-12 hour blocks. That means for most coaches, selling a client will equate to about $2,000 in revenue.

It's important to connect our goals with the things that are important to us in our lives. For example, "Make $2,000 a month in coaching income" is a good goal. But, "Make $2,000 a month in coaching income so that I can send my kids to private school" is better by far (assuming private school for your kids is important to you!).

In all my work with coaches, I've heard lots of coaching income goals. Things like:

- I want to make $2,000 a month so I can buy myself some things that don't fit into our family budget.
- I want to make $2,000 a month so I can take a vacation I've always dreamed of.
- I want to make $2,000 a month so I can take pressure off my spouse.
- I want to make $2,000 a month so I can give to causes that I care about.

This question is really only limited by the things you value, and there's no right or wrong answer. Give yourself permission to dream and see where it takes you!

It's important to have a goal. It's equally important to envision how achieving that goal will alter your life in a positive way!

A Note About $2,000:

There's a quick story about how I built my coaching business to being able to charge $200 an hour. When I was going through coach training with Mitch, I asked him how much he charged. He told me (at the time) he was charging $2,000 for 10 sessions over three months. In part due to my naivete and in part because I was committed to not holding myself back, I decided to charge $2,000 for my coaching packages, too. Perhaps I seem like an impudent kid at the time–and perhaps I was–thinking that I could just jump in at the top of the heap and skip past the work that it had taken Mitch to grow his business, his skills and his confidence.

But it wasn't JUST impudence at work. It was also a function of me learning from one of the best. You see, I "used" Mitch to get to 80% WAY faster that I could have if I hadn't had his help. I took a shorter road by building on his success. The 80/20 principle worked out. And you can do the same. There's no reason you can't get there just as quickly!

Take a few minutes to look at these journaling questions that will get you thinking about your own goals!

JOURNALING QUESTIONS:

What are some of the things you might do if someone gave you $2,000 in cash right now?

If you worked hard to earn that money, how might that change how you'd want to spend it?

What are some of the things that get you excited about additional income (along with additional impact and freedom) as you start your coaching adventure?

Part Three: 5 Question Asking Secrets

If you're this far in the book, it means that you are both excited about the concept of coaching itself AND you're open, if not excited, about the business side of coaching! That's fantastic!

It also means that you've been working hard on all these journaling questions. Since you've stuck with us, we want to give you a gift! These are five secrets to asking better coaching questions.

I like to call them the "Secret Strategies."

As you know, questions are a life coach's most important and powerful tool. We can ask questions that will open up possibilities for our clients. We can ask questions that help people see their situation from a different perspective and finally get "unstuck." We can ask questions to instill a sense of autonomy over the steps they will take which helps them OWN their plan and walk it out. Powerful questions play a critical role in how we bring value to our clients and help them finally achieve the breakthroughs and successes they've been wanting.

Our hope is that these five strategies will equip you as you continue to move toward either launching your new coaching practice or taking your current coaching business to the next level.

The beautiful thing about each of these strategies is that they are subtle. Most people won't even realize that you're using them. All they'll experience is the feeling of being safe as well as wanting to open up and share ideas. In fact, as you try these concepts, you might even have people say, "Wow. I'm not even sure why I'm telling you this." Or… "Gosh. You asked that one little question and I just talked for ten minutes!" These strategies will help you as you coach others, but you can also apply them to conversations with coworkers, friends and family. We've even had coaches tell us that they've used them to build trust and connection with TEENAGERS! Now that's saying something!

So we'll present each strategy, and as we do, I'll share some of the theory behind it and then offer some specific examples of each. We'll give you the opportunity to build some of your own coaching questions using these powerful concepts.

Secret Strategy 1: "Keep it Safe"

The first strategy we're going to explore is something we call "Keep it Safe."

If you boil down this approach, it's really all about asking a set of questions in an effective sequence. I'm not talking about principles of grammar here. I'm not talking about a complicated "sequence" like the launch of a NASA rocket.

- What I'm talking about is asking a series of simple but powerful questions in a way that:
- Helps make your coaching client feel safe
- Opens up possibilities
- Enables them to see things from a different perspective
- Allows them to learn from past experiences
- Empowers them to build a plan and take action

Let me ask you this. Have you ever asked a question and the person simply locked up? Maybe they looked back at you with a blank stare. Maybe you could hear the gears clanking away in their brain, but there was no response? Maybe you even saw a little puff of smoke coming out of their ear as their thinking came to a grinding halt?

I know I've experienced this, and when it happened I was tempted to think I was a bad coach or mentor. Other times I was tempted to think the person simply wasn't ready for the question. In hindsight, I realized that the reason, more often than not for the person's brain to seize up like an old Ford engine without oil, was that I'd asked the questions in the wrong sequence.

Sequence matters. That's why it's the focus of this first strategy.

We're not talking about a complicated sequence. You won't need a whiteboard or an excel spreadsheet to keep track of this sequence. Nope.

Want the sequence? Here it is:

Ask a "what" question. Then ask a "why" question.

That's it.

That's "Keep it Safe" in a nutshell.

"What" then "why."

Let me give you a few examples:

- What are a few of your goals for this next year?
- Why might it be good to pursue them now?

- What might some of your next steps be as you move closer to this goal?
- Why might those help in the process?
- What were some of the steps that you took with this project?
- Why do you think that worked?
- (Or... In hindsight, why do you think that didn't work?)
- What was something that got in the way?
- Why do you think that came up?

As you see these questions in the "what" then "why" sequence, ask yourself why you think that might work? Seriously... give it some thought. Why might that order make those questions more effective AND help you steer your coaching clients away from creative brain freeze?

You've probably already figured it out.

Here's the key: "Why" questions can be incredibly powerful. However, if you ask a "why" question too early it can put the person on the spot.

By asking a "what" question first and then asking a "why" question second, it's going to help your coachee to feel safe. This is important for a number of reasons.

If someone feels safe, they're going to be much more likely to open up to you. But more importantly, if they feel safe they will be more creative and they'll be able to learn a lot more from the situation. On the other hand, if they feel like they have to be on the defensive or feel like they have to explain themselves, then they will begin to shut down.

Let me give you an example to provide some context. Recently, I was helping one of my coaching clients. We were clear on a significant goal she wanted to accomplish, and we were starting to put together a plan. As we explored her options, I asked "What are some of the steps you might need to take to reach this goal?"

I listened and took notes as she listed out various steps she could take. I gave her room to get very creative and even have some fun with the list. Admittedly, some of the items got a little outlandish, but some of the crazier ideas seemed to fuel her innovative thinking so we went with it.

I followed that up with another "what" question to help to filter and prioritize our rather "creative" list of options. I asked "What might be the most important steps to take first?"

With this "what" question, she was able to sort through some of her ideas and really narrow the focus to three of the most important and timely tasks.

Then I followed up with a "why" question to bring it all home. I asked "Why might it be important for you to accomplish these tasks right now?"

She immediately responded with, "I've been think-ing about this goal for the last three years but something has been holding me back. I can tell you that I don't want to wake up three years from now and be in the same spot. So I've got to take action. In the past, I've tried to do too much right away, but now I know I need to start small but be really inten-tional. So I think these three things will help me get some quick wins. They'll also help me actually make some progress towards my goal!'

That response just flowed out of her. She didn't lock up. She didn't get creative brain freeze. It just came out. Although we were on the phone, I got the sense that a HUGE smile came over her face as it all played out. She felt safe and as a result she got creative. She also didn't feel like she had to defend her ideas so she could come at the list of to-dos from a place of ownership and excitement instead of feeling like she was having to argue for them.

Can you see the difference?

I expect you can.

It's subtle.

It's subtlety is why I missed this strategy when I was first starting as a coach. As you master this simple, powerful strategy, it's amazing to see what can happen. In addition to making your coaching client feel safe, there's another reason to ask a "what" question first and then a "why" question.

The "what" question allows people to be "situation focused."

The what question gets your client thinking about the situation. It gets them thinking about their process. It gets them thinking about their plan. It allows them to step into it and look around without the need to defend a specific approach or strategy right away.

If the "why" question comes too early, it can often put people on the defensive.

"Why do you want to do that?" Or... "Why is that important to you?"

A "why" question asked too early will put people up against a wall. Instead of inspiring them to be creative, we inspire them to defend their answer. A misplaced "why" might even spark a "fight-or-flight" type response that has them fighting for or scurrying away from possible solutions.

I'll give you another example to help illustrate what I mean.

I was working with a coaching client who was a successful entrepreneur. From the outset, I knew he really wanted to work on his "work-life balance," so we started there.

Right up front he shared that he'd tried a number of things in the past. He'd read books. He'd tried different apps. He'd gone to different workshops. Then he proceeded to say, "And that's why I'm not sure this is really going to work. I've tried all of these things but nothing's ever really stuck with me. I'm starting to be convinced that I'm 'kind of broken' and I'm always just going to be a little messed up on this front."

Though he was a little doubtful about his future success, it was good to hear his perspective. I wanted to get to the heart of the matter but also allow him to continue to feel safe enough to express his goals and his doubts. So I went with a "what" and "why" sequence.

I said, "All right, so what does 'work-life balance' actually mean to you? What does success look like in this case?" Then I got to hear his thoughts on this. He walked through what it actually meant to be "balanced" from his perspective. For him, it meant protected time with his family. It meant being in the moment and enjoying life. It meant being really effective at work so he could head home and not feel guilty. He also talked about what it didn't mean. He was clear that it didn't mean a life of ease. It didn't mean long hours of leisure time or life without hard work. In the end, we clarified what success looked like for him. It simply boiled down to the concept that when he was at work he wanted to fully focus on what he was doing there, but when he was home he wanted to fully focus on being home. That's "what" success looked like for him. Once we were clear on the "what," I went after the "why."

Next I asked him, "Why might that be important to you right now?"

I can tell you, he got really quiet.

We were on the phone, so I couldn't see him, but I'm guessing his eyes were getting a little misty. After a moment of silence he quietly said, "It's so important." He continued, "It's important to me, but it's even more important to my daughter. She's in high school, and if I don't get this right now, I'm gonna miss these last years of us being in the same house... being under the same roof. I just don't want to miss it."

At that point, I think he was ready to run through a brick wall to make his "what" a reality. His "why" had set in and all of a sudden balancing his time and being in the moment became both IMPORTANT and URGENT. Not because of something I said, but because he had uncovered both WHAT it was and WHY it was critical.

I'm confident that if I had started with a "why" question too early in our conversation (back when he was telling me about his doubts about time management) we would have wound up in a completely different place.

If I'd asked "why" questions like:

- Why are you doubtful?
- Why are you worried?
- Why hasn't it worked in the past?

I think it would have put him completely on the defensive. He would have either had to defend those failures or those past bad experiences, or he would have had to defend his lifestyle up to this point. When I allowed him to first see the "what" clearly and followed that with the "why," it helped him to get clear and then commit at a much deeper level.

Asking a what question first and asking a why question second helps keep things safe, it helps them see clearly, it helps them go deeper and oftentimes, it helps them commit. That's the "Keeping it Safe" strategy.

Let's get you an assignment so you can go deeper and own this idea.

JOURNALING QUESTIONS:

ROUND ONE:

Try out this sequence as a journaling exercise. Ask yourself some "what" questions:

What are some of the things about coaching that I find the most interesting, intriguing, exciting, inspiring?

What are some of those things about coaching that get me the most excited?

Then follow up with a few "why" questions:

Why are these things important?

Why is it important to help others in this way?

ROUND TWO:

Review these sample "Keep it Safe" questions and modify two to better fit your clients and/or your world.

What were some of the steps that you took with this project?

Why do you think that worked? (Or... In hindsight, why do you think that didn't work?)

What was something that got in the way?

Why do you think that came up?

What is something that we could do to improve this process?

Why might that work? Why might that be important to try?

What is something you'd really like to focus on for the next three months?

Why might that be important to you?

Why might that be important to _____?

YOUR MODIFIED QUESTION 1:

YOUR MODIFIED QUESTION 2:

Secret Strategy 2: Inspire Stories

As we ask more powerful coaching question, one thing I think you'll realize is that we're not talking about huge, sweeping changes. Often the change is something very simple. That's definitely the case with this next strategy.

This next strategy we call "Inspire Stories."

The strategy focuses on solely changing one word.

The Strategy: Instead of asking someone to explain something, ask them to describe it.

I know that might sound almost too subtle, but I suspect you can already begin to hear the difference. Let me give you an example of how it can work. As you're coaching someone, let's say that you're really wanting them to learn from an experience they had in the past week.

If you say, "Explain what happened," what does that do? For most people, that statement puts them on the defensive. (You might even feel that intuitively as you read that sentence or imagine someone asking you that question.) It makes them feel like they have to defend what it is that they did or tried. If they feel like they're back is against the wall, it will be very difficult for them to learn from what happened.

However, the word describe can move them into what we call "story mode."

For example, you could say, "Describe what happened when you made that change this week."

Just by seeing the two examples, can you feel the difference?

The word "describe" will help your coaching client move into more descriptive language. From an experience standpoint, it allows them to step into the experience and look around a bit. It enables them to say, "Okay, well this happened, and that happened." It even frees them up to talk about their personal experience. They might respond with, "I was really nervous as I was getting ready, but once I stepped into that role I really connected with it."

The difference between using the word "explain" and replacing it with "describe" really changes that experience for your coaching clients. It's subtle but I've certainly seen it help people open up.

Some additional examples could be:

- "Describe what your thought process was as you worked through that problem."
- "Describe what it was like to do the home-work last week."
- "Describe what it felt like to get that task completed."

Another place that I love to use a "describe question" is when we're kicking off a coaching session. I like to ask, "Describe something that went well this past week." Now they might say, "Oh gosh, nothing went well. I didn't get as much done as I wanted to. I got busy and I got off track."

If they respond in this way, I'll usually say something like, "We'll get to some of those things in a second, but describe at least one thing that went well." Now, sometimes they might even just say, "You know, uh, at least I just did something, I did finally schedule that meeting, which I've been pushing off for months!"

For example, I had one client that was trying some new things and at the beginning of a follow up call I said, "So, describe something that went well this past week." She said, "Oh gosh, it didn't go well at all." I said, "I hear you. Sometimes it's easy to focus on the things that didn't go the way we planned. Don't worry. We'll dig into that in a second. For now, describe something that went well."

After a pause, she started to list some of the things that actually did go well. As she walked me through this list, she realized by the end, she had really gotten a lot done. In fact, she said, "Wow. When I look back, I got about 80 to 90% of my list done, but that last 10 to 20% was just staring me in the face! I forgot all the good stuff." As you can imagine, this was pretty revealing!

Plus, as she was describing some of the things she had done, she recognized that she'd had some fun accomplishing those tasks. She even remembered feeling a sense of peace one evening after a long day because she was finally taking action on her big goals and dreams. Finally, she brought up a mid-week epiphany that she was actually living in the moment while she was with her kids instead of beating herself up for not working longer that day.

Sure, at first she wanted to list the things she hadn't done. But when I asked her to describe some of the things she HAD done, she completely moved into story mode which gave her permission to explore it, learn from the experiences at a different level and celebrate the wins along the way, too.

That's why I want to give you this strategy. It's a subtle shift but it is oh so powerful.

Now, I encourage you to start experimenting with it. Like last time, I want you to experience it first and then design some "describe" questions yourself.

JOURNALING QUESTIONS:

ROUND ONE:

Try a few "describe" questions as a journaling exercise.

Describe a time when you really felt like you were coaching someone. Describe what it felt like to help them. What were a few things you really enjoyed about that process?

Describe what it would feel like to get to that on a more regular basis.

ROUND TWO:

See the list of questions below. Modify a few and put them in your own language to make them a better fit for you:

Describe how this played out.

Describe what seemed to work.

Describe what seemed to break down.

Describe your thought process as you worked through that problem.

Describe what your next steps might be.

YOUR MODIFIED QUESTION 1:

YOUR MODIFIED QUESTION 2:

Secret Strategy 3: Consult Thyself

(AKA: The "Mother-in-Law Question")

As you can tell, these strategies are pretty simple, but they can be wildly powerful. This one is no different. In fact, I have to admit that of all of them, this one is probably my favorite.

This strategy is the one we call "Consult Thyself."

It's framing questions so as to help people advise themselves. It works especially well for someone who has run out of ideas or for the person who feels stuck. Maybe they feel like they really don't have anything else to offer, and they're starting to shut down. They feel like they just don't have any solutions.

When this happens, it's really tempting to just jump in and start offering ideas. (Maybe you've already experienced this.) Sometimes jumping in and saving the day feels good and also seems to keep things moving along. BUT that's also when their Intellectual Immune System starts to kick in. Remember this concept from earlier in the book? It's the concept that we tend to reject ideas which come from the outside but embrace ideas that we feel like we've had a hand in creating.

The "Consult Thyself" strategy can assist in navigating that. It helps someone create a solution they can genuinely own. The idea behind this strategy is to encourage them to look at their situation from a different angle rather than the coach merely offering a solution. As you do this, you can help them discover a new approach, and as they exercise this strategy, they will OWN the solution.

Although we officially call this strategy "Consult Thyself," my team also affectionately refers to this concept as the "Mother-In-Law Question" because of a something that happened at a LIVE training awhile back.

A few years ago we had a group of new coaches in for a certification. As a part of the training, we rolled out this strategy on a Friday. That night everyone went back to their hotel rooms to rest up for the next day. On Saturday morning one of the participants came in early with an ear-to-ear smile and said, "I've got to give you a hug." I said, "I'll always take that, but why do I get a hug this morning?" She explained, "Well, I used the 'Consult Thyself' on my mother-in-law last night." With me wondering how it unfolded, she continued, "It worked! Thank you!"

She explained she'd gotten a call from her mother-in-law when she got back to her hotel room. As it turned out, there was a challenge within the family and her sister-in-law was having some troubles. As this new coach listened, her mother-in-law said she just wanted to call her daughter and "fix" the situation, but this participant knew that getting advice from her mother-in-law probably wasn't going to work. She imagined her sister-in-law's Intellectual Immune System kicking into high gear as the advice poured out. In the same way, this new coach also knew that it would be really hard to offer her mother-in-law advice on the matter. Ironically, she recognized that if she offered a solution in this high-tension situation, her mother-in-law's Intellectual Immune System would probably reject it too.

She thought, "Mitch told us to experiment with this stuff we're learning. The 'Consult Thyself' might just work here." She tried it.

Her mind raced and she remembered her mother-in-law had a friend who had a daughter with some of the same challenges. She said, "Hey, mom, doesn't your friend Marci have a daughter that's kind of going through the same thing?" Her mother-in-law said, "Yes, yes I do." Then the new coach took the next step in the process. She said, "Mom, what would you tell Marci to do if she asked you for advice? Would you tell her to go and "fix" it for her daughter?"

After she asked these questions it got really quiet on the other end of the line. Then her mother-in-law said, "Gosh, no. No, that would be the last thing I'd tell her to do. That would never work." It got quiet again. Something clicked and the mother-in-law simply said, "Hmmmm. I just need to give her some space, don't I?" The new coach let that hang in the air for a minute. Then she replied, "Yes, if you think that's the best thing to do...I agree with you."

And that's how it works. This simple strategy enabled the coach to help her mother-in-law discover a plan that she could own, and as a result, she was able to walk it out. We see this work in similar ways with many of our coach graduates that use this strategy in their own practices. It works because if the client discovers a solution, they own it, and if they own it, they're exponentially more likely to walk it out.

Here are some other examples of how you might apply this "Consult Thyself" strategy.

Maybe a coaching client is getting ready to try something new. You could ask questions like:

"Hey, what advice would you give somebody that's looking to do the same thing?"

I did this recently with a client who was considering paddle boarding as a means of exercise. (He was working on some work/life balance strategies.) He'd never done anything like this before and was feeling a little insecure about it. So I asked, "What would you tell someone else to do if they were thinking about getting started with paddle boarding?" It was interesting because even though this client was starting to feel locked up and even though he'd NEVER gone paddle boarding before, he had some ideas for me. He said, "Well gosh, I'd probably tell them to take some lessons. Yeah, that's a good idea. Maybe go to a surf shop, to find out how to do that. And I'd definitely say that they shouldn't buy a board until they knew they really liked it. But I know you can rent them so that's not a big deal. But that way it would really eliminate all the risk that would go along with it." After he was done giving this "advice," he got quiet. Then he said, "Wow. I guess I have my plan then." And we both laughed.

Maybe it's something with your client's work. Maybe it's something that they want to try that's new for them. Sometimes I'll say, "What advice would you give an intern if they were trying this for the first time?" Or… "What if somebody on your team was trying to take this to the next level? What advice might you give them?" This simply helps them to look at it from a different angle and it opens up possibilities. In some way they give themselves permission to look at the situation from a little different vantage point and all of a sudden they're full of ideas.

This can work in a lot of different ways.

In fact, I'll tell a little personal story of how I used this strategy on myself. Recently, my family and I were working on a home improvement project in our basement. One morning I needed to move a long bookshelf that stands at one end of our family room. It's made of oak and it's heavy. Being a guy, I didn't want to ask for help, and I also didn't want to clear everything off this bookshelf. I just wanted to get it done quickly and heck, I just needed to move it about two feet! I thought, "I've got this." But when

I went to lift it, I promptly realized I could barely get it to budge. In fact, I was only able to lift it about an inch off the ground and thought, "I'm gonna either get a hernia, or I'm going to waste a lot of time finding someone else to help me with this."

So, I sat and I thought and then took the "Consult Thyself" approach. I asked myself the question, "If I was going to give advice to someone else, what would I tell them to do?" And then my thoughts went to a different set of questions. I asked myself, "Who else has done something like this? Who could I be learning from? Who else has moved big heavy objects without a crane or a lot of help?"

My brain started to race as I thought through it. Then it hit! Do you know what came to mind? It might surprise you. All of a sudden my mind went racing back to my childhood Encyclopedia Britannica collection. Do you remember that? Ohhhhh all of those encyclopedias lined up on a shelf. Then my mind's eye went to the "E" edition. Why? Because I remember looking through that as a kid, and one of the pictures in there was of the Egyptians, and how they would move those huge blocks as they were building the pyramids. Then I remembered what was underneath those big blocks! It was big logs that they'd made smooth and round. As a result, they were able to roll those huge blocks with just a few people pushing them. (Do you remember that picture? Maybe you had the same collection of Encyclopedia Britannica.) But all of a sudden a solution popped into my brain.

"Egyptians! They moved big stuff, and they did it without cranes!" Then a series of ideas came very rapidly to me, and I found a wooden dowel I had on my workbench. Next, I cut the dowel into three short pieces. Finally, I asked our sons to help me. As I lifted that heavy bookshelf up an inch or so, our youngest son got down and put those three small wooden dowels underneath it. Then that big oak bookcase rolled like it was on greased ball bearings! As a result of the "Consult Thyself" strategy, I was able to get the job done in about ten minutes! (That's right! I moved like an Egyptian in the process!)

So yes! I'd actually used the strategy on myself and it worked! I'd consulted myself by saying, "Alright, who else has done something like this?" I can tell you that I went from stuck to having that bookshelf moved in just a few minutes! Sometimes it's as simple as encouraging people to give themselves advice, and that process can start opening new possibilities.

I'm not sure where you are. Maybe you're excited about the idea of becoming a coach or taking your coaching practice to the next level. Maybe you could use this strategy yourself. Think about it. What if you gave yourself a little advice? Maybe you're feeling a little stuck? Maybe you get excited about becoming a coach, but then feel a little overwhelmed at all of the different things that you think you should be doing.

What if you took time to journal a response to a

question using this strategy?

What if you were to give advice to someone who wants to build a successful and sustainable coaching practice? I know you may not feel like you know everything you need to know yet. That's okay. But what advice would you give to somebody who's a few months behind you in this process? What are some of the things you've learned so far? What are some of the things you guess you'd need to do? What if you gave yourself the opportunity to "consult thyself?"

Take that opportunity and just see where it takes you!

JOURNALING QUESTIONS:

ROUND ONE:

Consult thyself; experience the power of this simple little strategy and see where it takes you.

What advice would you give to somebody who is a year behind you in this process?

What might you tell them to do as they're getting ready for this journey of starting a coaching practice?

ROUND TWO:

Take a look at these sample "Consult Thyself" questions below and modify two to better fit you. Change the wording or change the context to make them work for you.

What would you tell your friend to do if they were in this situation?

What advice would you give an intern if they were trying to solve this?

What advice would you give Kim if she was trying to _____ ?

If someone was trying to experiment with how to put this into a better sequence, what might be a good first step?

What might _____ do if they were facing the same situation?

If a brand new manager was facing this situation, what would be a few things you'd want to remind them?

Think of a good leader that you've had. What might they do in this situation?

YOUR MODIFIED QUESTION 1:

YOUR MODIFIED QUESTION 2:

Secret Strategy 4: Body of Evidence

This next strategy is a tool for your coaching tool-box that you'll be able to pull out when a client is struggling with their confidence. Maybe they're entering into a time in which they're going to try something new, or maybe they're dealing with a setback, and their confidence has been rocked a little bit.

It is something we call the "Body of Evidence" approach. It helps your coaching clients reflect and build a body of evidence that will allow them to know "I can push through this."

Not only that, it also enables them to think of past experiences and learn from them and apply that knowledge in the here and now.

One of my favorite examples for this approach comes from a time when I was working with a client who wanted to launch a business. Granted, that's a pretty big endeavor, and he had never been an entrepreneur before… I mean, ever! Frankly, I could totally identify with him. His story was a lot like mine. He didn't have any entrepreneurs in his family line so it was pretty overwhelming, and almost everything he was having to do felt new. (Can you identify?) During one of our coaching sessions, he was feeling a little frustrated and tired. In fact, I could tell that he was wondering whether he should even continue with this dream.

It was at this point that I tried the "Body of Evidence" approach.

I said, "Can you think of a time when you needed to learn something new... and you did it?"

He was quiet for a minute as he was thinking. Then he said, "I... I don't know."

Then I said, "How about from when you were a kid? Was there ever a time when you had to learn something new?" He thought back, "I actually had to learn how to fish." Honestly, I was expecting him to talk about riding a bike or something like that. But I went with it. I said, "Okay. How did that go?" He replied, "Well, it may sound weird, but I had to first learn how to fish. See my dad was a fisherman and my uncles were fishermen." But then he trailed off for a minute and thought. He continued, "I tried to avoid fishing for a while because I really wasn't all that into worms and hooks. Heck, the stuff they used kind of scared and overwhelmed me. There were so many different options. I remember just looking at my dad's tackle box and my head would spin."

When he paused, I just encouraged him by saying, "Okay, yes. This is a great example. Then what happened?"

He continued, "Well, I finally just kind of confided in my dad. I let him know that I wanted to get started, but I just don't know how." That's a pretty big step for a little kid, but as it turned out his dad was great. It sounds like he got excited about his son's interest but also promised to slow down the next time they went out to fish.

So, the next weekend they went fishing… just the two of them. As they got started, instead of over-whelming him with everything in that huge tackle box, his dad just took out the simplest hook and put a worm on it. He even showed him a simple two-step approach for doing that. The rest of the day, he said his dad just took it one step at a time. At one point, he showed him how to tie that simple hook onto his line. A little later he showed him how to cast. Then they just sat together on that sunny, lazy summer day and waited. Lo and behold, after about an hour and a half of sitting, fzzz! Finally, a fish grabbed that hook, and made a run for it. You could hear the joy in my client's voice as he remem-bered that experience with his dad. He even said, "The minute that fish was hooked… so was I!" He instantly fell in love with fishing. He said, "I fought that thing for a few minutes. Heck, I almost believed I'd caught a shark! As it turned out, it was only a little, itty-bitty fish. It almost looked like one of the goldfish in my tank at home! But, man, it was great. I felt so excited. And by the end of the day not only was I tying my own hooks and working with worms, but I'd already experimented with one or two other things that were in that magical tackle box of my dad's."

I jumped in to say, "That's such a great story. I love it. What would you say you learned from that expe-rience that you might be able to apply here?" He thought for a minute and then replied, "I just learned I had to take it one step at a time. Yeah, that was one of the things my dad just kept telling me. Just take it one step at a time."

"That's great. What else?" I said.

"Well, right. When I was first thinking about getting started with fishing, I was feeling all the same feelings I'm feeling now: frustrated, overwhelmed and feeling like I don't know what I need to know but at the same time...I also feel excited about the whole thing. Now that I think about it...with fishing, I guess all I needed to do was to ask for some help and just start taking it one step at a time. That's probably what I should do here too...huh?"

I said, "Ohhhhh I agree."

So, he built on his own body of evidence. He recognized that he'd never been an entrepreneur before, but at the same time, he'd never been a fisherman before that summer day with his dad. He is now a great fisherman who has fished all over the world. That memory helped him re-engage and go after his dream of being an entrepreneur. We simply started taking his lessons from fishing and applying them to starting his business. We explored whom he could lean on to get input and ideas. We talked about ways he could take it one step at a time. We even discussed ways to make sure he enjoyed the journey, too!

So let me give you some different examples of how this question might look, and how you might use it.

FACING ADVERSITY:

In a case in which a client is facing some challenges, you could say, "Think of a time when you've faced something similar." After asking, you just let them sit. Sometimes the memory might come immediately. It might only take a nanosecond and they'll remember something. Other times it may take them a little while. If that's the case, just give them that freedom to sit and think. Once they have a thought, you can follow up with, "Tell me about it." Or… "Describe it for me." Or… "What was that like?"

After they've told you about the experience, you could ask, "Okay, how might you take what you learned from that and apply it to this situation?" Then listen as they talk through how the lessons learned might just apply to the here and now.

As you listen, hone in on those things you want to reinforce. It might be things they say, or simply observations you hear that they might be missing. For example, I had a client who was frustrated with a friend who was supposed to be helping them with a goal. After talking about it for a minute, I asked her if she could remember a time when she'd been frustrated with someone but handled the situation really well. After a moment or two, she came back with a story. I listened for specifics and reflected those back to my client by saying, "Okay, if I'm hearing you right, you first really listened to that person before laying into them. Once you did that, you realized they misunderstood what you'd asked them to do. That's great! It sounds like that really helped in that situation. But before the conversation even happened, it also sounds like you took a walk around the block to blow off some steam and get some perspective. If I'm understanding your approach, that really helped you move into the conversation with a more level head."

So I simply restated parts of her story that might help in her current situation.

As you listen and reflect, you can even help them learn from situations that didn't end well. If they respond with a story that ended poorly, you can continue the discussion by asking, "Knowing what you know now, what's something that you would want to do differently if you had the chance to walk out that situation again?" Or... "If you had a do-over button and could face that situation again, what would you do differently?"

Whether they remember a situation that went well or a situation that had a "less than ideal" outcome, you can still ask "Body of Evidence" questions. As you do, you'll be able to build that body of evidence they can rely on, be bolstered by or learn from.

As you think through the strategy, I want to give you a "Body of Evidence" question to think through. Maybe you're excited about coaching, or really excited about where this is going, but maybe you're feeling a little stuck. Maybe you're feeling a little overwhelmed by all the things you have to learn. What I'd like to do is ask you a question…

Journaling Questions:

ROUND ONE:

Think back to a time when you had to learn something new. What were some things you did to make that work?

What were some things you did that helped your journey? Think through this and write your responses below.

ROUND TWO:

Take a look at the sample "Body of Evidence" questions below and develop two of them in your own words.

Examples:

Tell me about a time when you faced something similar?

[After listening] How might you apply what you learned there... to this situation?

Describe a time when you felt _____ before.

[After listening] What was something you did to deal with it?

[After listening] What part of that solution could you apply here?

YOUR MODIFIED QUESTION 1:

YOUR MODIFIED QUESTION 2:

Secret Strategy 5: The "Power of Might"

Our fifth strategy complements all the others.

In fact, as you hear about it, you'll see how we have already woven it into many of the other strategies. It's so subtle, yet powerful. This is actually one of the most powerful concepts you will have at your disposal. It's so powerful we call this strategy the "Power of Might."

First, I want to say that this is something which is applicable for anyone you're coaching, but it's especially appropriate for anyone who deals with perfectionism.

I will admit "I'm Mitch Matthews and I am a recovering perfectionist." Yes, that's right. I'm a "perfectionist in recovery." How about you? Maybe, like me, you deal with some perfectionistic challenges a little bit…or a lot.

Before we move into the specific strategy, let's take a moment to look at perfectionism because it impacts more people than you might think. A lot of people wrestle with perfectionism, but they just don't know that's what they're dealing with. When most envision a "perfectionist," they assume the person's work desk looks like a finely designed laboratory with everything in its place, or the perfectionist's home looks like a museum with everything perfectly designed and organized.

The truth, however, is most perfectionists tend to be "pile people." Why? Well, oftentimes a perfectionist receives a letter, a note or a memo, but they think to themselves, "Oh, I don't have a perfect place to put this. I'll just set it here for now, and I'll put it away when I find the right place." But then what happens? Maybe a few hours or a few days later, the next piece of paper comes... and where does it go? You know where. Right on top of that last note. The pile continues to grow until it gets moved somewhere to make room for that new important piece of paper.

Can you identify?

What's also interesting is that perfectionists often get misdiagnosed as "procrastinators." That's because a perfectionist will be VERY effective at starting a project and getting it to 80-90%, but then they get locked up. It's so hard to push past that last 10 to 20% because it's just not "perfect" yet. So they need a deadline to push them over that line. It takes the pressure of the clock ticking to force them to say, "It's not perfect, but it's got to be done!" And they hit send... just in the nick of time.

Again, can you identify with that?

If you can't... bless you! I envy you. But if you can, then know you're not alone. MANY people deal with perfectionist tendencies and just don't know it. As a coach it's really important to be aware that people might get hit with perfectionism as you ask them questions.

This strategy will help everyone, but it will especially help my brothers and sisters in P.A. (Perfectionists Anonymous.)

It's based on the concept that if you strive for absolutes too early in the process, you can really shut down someone's creativity. By asking them questions that force them to get too specific too early, you can lock them up and limit their thinking.

Let me give you a non-coaching example that might be helpful. Let's say you're talking to a friend and they ask you, "Hey, what's your favorite comedy of all time?" Have you ever been asked a question like this? (Or maybe it was, "What's your favorite song?" Or… "What's your favorite movie?") Did you lock up? Did your brain spin trying to land on your "favorite" right away? That's what happens to most people.

In this situation, the reason most people lock up is because the person asking the question is trying to move you to absolutes while you're needing to be creative first. Not only are you trying to think about all the comedies you've seen, but now you're also trying to decide which one of those is the best. Suddenly you're locked up.

Have you experienced this? I'm betting you have. If

so, it was because you were shooting for an absolute before you allowed your brain to be creative.

"Might" allows you to switch up that order. It enables people to be creative first and selective second.

For a coaching-specific example, let's say a coach is working with someone who needs to develop a plan to achieve a goal. They know their client needs to make some good decisions and start strong. As a result, the coach asks, "What's the best first step you could take?" Or, "What's your best move here?" It's understandable that a coach doesn't want to waste any time and they want their client to develop the best plan possible, but can you imagine the client's mental gears grinding to a halt? That client is now not only thinking about what their next steps might be, but at the same time they're trying to quickly determine which is the best. This is why people often look back at new coaches with a blank, confused stare. Their brains are trying to process too much, too quickly.

When you're helping someone develop something like a plan, there is a two-step process that needs to happen. The first step is helping them think through their options and THEN think through prioritizing and weighing out those options. Think CREATIVE first, and SELECTIVE second. So, when a coach asks for their "best first step" they are skipping to the second step too early. The "Power of Might" strategy helps you avoid rushing the process. It enables you to help your client explore

their options before making the call on which
is best.

Now, let me give you a "Power of Might" example to
help show the difference.

Instead of saying, "What's the next step?" or
"What's your best step here?"

A coach could ask, "What might be a next step in
this situation?" Or... "What might you do next?"

Can you feel the difference?

It's subtle, but if you're on the receiving end of a
"Might" question, I'm betting you could almost feel
your creativity start to open up. A "Might" question gives you the ability to say, "Let's consider
the options first, and then we'll decide on the right
move second."

It's amazing. There have been so many times when
I've been working with a coaching client, and all
of a sudden they'll say, "Okay, well, I feel like I'm
out of ideas." Then I'll throw out a "Power of Might"
question like: "Okay, well I understand you're feeling locked up. I hear you on that. I've sure been
there. What might be on the list of things you could
do next?"

Often times, that "might" helps them to loosen up.
It helps them to explore their options again, without

having to make a call on specifics too early. I'll even allow them to list out some things we've talked about before, but that even tends to spark some new CREATIVITY.

Then, I'll shift gears and start to move into getting SELECTIVE. I'll say, "Okay, this is a good list. What might the next step be?"

Notice, I'm still using a "might" question as we start the selection process. I'll stay with it. "Okay, good. After that, what might your next step be?"

More often than not, they'll go from being locked up to having ideas pour out and then having them ranked in order before they even knew what hit them. Again, it's subtle but so powerful.

The "Power of Might" will help your clients tap into their CREATIVITY first and their SELECTIVITY second!

I'm pretty confident that you're tracking with me. So now, you know what's next. I want you to experiment with the "Power of Might." Answer the journalling questions below and experience the Power of Might first hand. Then in ROUND TWO, create some "Power of Might" questions yourself.

JOURNALING QUESTIONS:

ROUND ONE:

As you think about this next year, what might be some things you'd like to experience? (These can totally be professional, personal, emotional, spiritual, or... whatever.)

What goals might you want to achieve in this next year?

(These can totally be professional, personal, emotional, spiritual, or... whatever.)

After creating your lists of experiences and goals, what might be your top two to three of each? What might be most important? List the top items below.

ROUND TWO:

Take a look at these sample "Power of MIGHT" questions below and develop two in your own words.

Examples:

- What might be a good next step in this situation?
- What might be a solution here?
- What might be a solution here?
- [After listening] Now that you've come up with some possible solutions, which do you like best? Which would you want to try first?
- What might you want to focus on next?
- [After listening] Of these ideas... which one would you want to try first?

YOUR MODIFIED QUESTION 1:

YOUR MODIFIED QUESTION 2:

The Journey Continues...

Congratulations!

If you're here... it means you read through these first ten questions and realized coaching could be a fantastic fit for you! That's no small feat! (Plus, you dug into our "Secret Strategies" to take your ability to ask powerful coaching questions to the next level! Well done!)

You should know that as the popularity of the Coach Mindset has grown, we have offered these ten critical questions to thousands of people around the world to help them decide if coaching is right for them. As we have, some people have asked if we are trying to talk people out of becoming a coach with these questions.

In fact, one person sent an email and said, "Most coach training programs are pounding me with marketing and sales pitches, but you guys are just helping me clarify whether I really want to be a coach or not. It's been super helpful, and I've appreciated the fact that you haven't been trying to sell me. But at some point, are you going to try to sell me on being a part of the Coach Mindset?"

I thought that was great! We got back to them to ensure them that we'd let them know whatever they wanted to know about the Coach Mindset and invite them to be a part of the next wave of training when it was offered. BUT our main goal with information like this is to help people:

- Decide whether coaching is right for them
- Build their confidence so they can move forward and take action
- Launch a successful and sustainable coaching practice

I'll be the first to admit that when some people thought through these ten questions... they realized that coaching was a bad fit! One or more of the questions made them think, "Wow, coaching just isn't for me."

Sometimes people have realized they don't have a group of people they are passionate about helping. Or sometimes people come to understand that they wouldn't be able to be quiet and listen to their clients. And some people just admit that they're not willing to work hard to make their dream of coaching a reality.

When that happens, it's not a bad thing. It's a good thing. It's good for a person to realize that they wouldn't be an effective coach. It's good because it saves them a lot of time and money. It's good because it also frees them up to pursue other things.

BUT... for those people who really connected with these questions... it's helped them move forward with confidence and finally take action!

If you've made it this far, I'm guessing you're saying, "YES! It's time! It's finally time!"

So we say, "Well done!"

You've had to work hard to get to this place, AND you're a special kind of person if these questions helped confirm that becoming a successful life or business coach is the right fit for you!

Now, the journey continues.

For some, you could start to coach people right away.

For some, you will be able to take your experience (along with our 5 Powerful Question strategies) and get started.

If that's you…great! Go for it.

BUT… for most. You need some additional training.

That was certainly what I needed!

When I was first getting started, I had some sales experience, and I'd done some speaking and workshop facilitation. Plus, I'd just seemed to coach and mentor countless friends, family members and co-workers over my lifetime.

However, I knew I needed help to:

- Grow my confidence in coaching with effective strategies and tools
- Learn a process for consistently taking people through a set of steps that brought value and break through
- Understand the business of coaching—everything from contracts and brochures to marketing and actually getting paid
- Know how to launch my business efficiently so I could do it on the side while I worked my full-time job
- Master the concepts I'd need to implement to not only start a coaching practice but to also make it successful and sustainable so it could be my full time job!

(Maybe you can identify with those goals.)

That's what I set out to do.

I found a training that helped me get started. It was a solid program which really helped me grow in my coaching expertise, however, it didn't introduce any business concepts... at all.

Consequently, I emerged from the training with more confidence in my coaching abilities but still completely lost when it came to the business side of coaching.

As a result, honestly, I floundered. I felt lost. I had numerous botched starts.

I spent too much on a website. I started to attend every networking meeting known to man and became exhausted in the process. I tried to serve EVERYONE but wound up helping NO ONE. It was brutal.

In fact, I almost quit numerous times.

But hey, looking back…it was understandable. I was tired. I was overwhelmed. I was scared. And… frankly I was embarrassed that things just weren't seeming to work. (Ever been there?)

Then… by the grace of God, a LOT of studying of business strategies, some good advice and a LOT of hard work… things started to click. I put a two-year plan in place to build my practice to a place where it could become my full-time job. But within five months of walking out that plan… I was able to quit my job and start coaching and speaking full time! That's right. After five months, I was able to call my manager in that "bad fit" job and let him know I was quitting to pursue my dream!

And I have never looked back!

I'm also wildly blessed to say that I've had times in which I've made more in ONE MONTH than I used to make in ONE YEAR in my old "safe" corporate job. Yes. I'm wildly blessed.

Here's the deal. I don't bring that up to brag. I share that to inspire you to stay on this journey. I'm not promising you that it's going to be fast, and I'm not saying that it's going to be easy.

But it will be incredibly rewarding, and, to steal a phrase from the Peace Corps, I can tell you that it will be hard work that you'll LOVE!

I also want to encourage you to learn from my mistakes.

As you think about investing in coach training, make sure you choose coach training that includes both COACH TRAINING and BUSINESS TRAINING!

This is exactly why we designed the Coach Mindset–Elite Life Coach Training and Certification the way we did. When we first launched it back in 2008, I didn't want people to have to face the same battles I did. I wanted to equip them with the best and most effective coach training AND the best and easiest to implement business concepts. That way our coach graduates could not only start helping people right away, but... if they wanted to... could also launch a coaching practice that would be successful and sustainable! (And a whole lot of fun!)

That's what I want to encourage you to do!

Find a coach training program that's the right fit for you, and make sure that it includes coach training

AND business training.

If you'd like to find out more about our LIVE and online training programs, you can go here to find out more. (http://trainingtobealifecoach.com/category/certification-information/)

Obviously, we're not the only program out there but we would LOVE to help you to become the coach you want to be!

If you would like to find out more about the Coach Mindset, we'd be ecstatic to let you know about courses like our "Scientific Method Coaching Model"™ which gives our graduates a step-by-step approach to coach their clients effectively and with confidence. Many have been able to charge coaching rates of $1,500 to $6,000 as a result! Plus, we offer a course called Successful Coach Blueprint™ which provides you with a step-by-step approach to branding and marketing your coaching practice so that you can connect with your ideal clients and avoid "bad fit" clients. Most importantly, whether it's coaching strategies or business principles, we boil it down so you only get the most important content. You won't be overwhelmed. Rather, you'll emerge with a clear plan that will enable you to build a successful and sustainable coaching practice.

Yes. We would be honored to get to help you on this journey and walk along side you as you build the life and the business you've always wanted! Simply check out (http://trainingtobealifecoach.com/category/certification-information/) to find out more.

Finally, whether you choose the Coach Mindset or another program, know that we're rooting for you!

There's a HUGE need for coaches because so many people need help living more of the life they were created to live!

So... get out there, help others and do what YOU were put on the planet to do!

Download the AudioBook and Action Guide Free

Just to say thanks for downloading our book, we would like to give you the full audiobook and action guide journal 100% free!

visit http://trainingtobealifecoach.com/action

45359261R00088

Made in the USA
San Bernardino, CA
07 February 2017